Martin Quigley, an angler and environmentalist, grew up in Clonmel but now lives in County Kilkenny. He began writing at an early age but diverted to pursue studies in the visual arts. A graduate of Crawford College of Art, Cork, and the University of Ulster, his work has been widely exhibited and commissioned. He currently lectures in art and design at Waterford Institute of Technology.

A river seems a magic thing. A magic, moving, living part of the earth itself –
for it is from the soil, both from its depth and from its surface,
that a river has its beginnings.
Laura Gilpin (1891-1979) *The Rio Grande*, Introduction (1949)

A man is blessed a thousand times over to be born near a river.
It sings to him every day.

John B. Keane

Acknowledgements

Edward Power, my most exacting and sensitive editor. You felt it and lived it, and never doubted.

Michael Coady, who gave me directions, and said, drive on.

Mary Shortt, who opened a sluice gate to let me flow.

Marian, Liam, Seamus and Josephine, for helping and keeping my spirits up.

Thank you.

Dedication

To Marian, Cathal and Muireann.
Liam, Eileen and Hilary,
who drift with me each day in different ways

Drifting with the River Gods

Martin Quigley

The Collins Press

Published in 2003 by
The Collins Press
West Link Park,
Doughcloyne,
Wilton,
Cork

Martin Quigley has asserted his right to be identified as author of this work.

British Library Cataloguing in Publication data.

Quigley, Martin
    Drifting with the river gods
    1. Quigley, Martin - Childhood and youth 2. Fishing - Ireland
    - Suir River 3. poaching - Ireland - Suir River - 4. Suir River
    (Ireland)
    I. Title
    941.9'10823'092

    ISBN 1903464420

Cover image: M. Coady
Cover design: Edit+

Printed in the Ireland by Woodprintcraft

Typesetting by The Collins Press

Chapter 1

Wiggles at the Bow

It was The Boy's eleventh summer, and he felt poised on the threshold of great adventure. He lay back amidships and watched his Uncle Paddy pole the tar-black, flat-bottomed boat out around mid-river, to drift in the moderate currents. Fingers of light stroked the weeds on the gravelly bottom and, every so often, startled trout darted away. Wiggles, their liver-and-white springer spaniel, planted his front paws firmly on the gunnel and made a gallant figurehead. For as long as The Boy could remember, Wiggles had been part of everything. He was an old hand, well-schooled in the ways of the fly-fisherman. Ten seasons plying the Suir with Paddy Whelan and his companions made him river-wise, yet he kept the curiosity and excitement of his puppy days. The slightest movement, perhaps a twig, or a leaf on the water, set his squat tail wagging recklessly.

Ten is old for a dog. By human reckoning, Wiggles should have been as old and wizened as Nogger Brown in the battered caravan behind the family house that was crumbling even when Nogger was a boy. Wiggles seemed as bright and lively as ever. Wise as an old river-dog, and playful as a puppy. Uncle Paddy used his hand like a teller's visor and looked towards Gashouse Bridge.

A heat haze hung over the water and blurred the four elegant sandstone arches. Each winter, Gashouse Bridge defied marauding floods, and when summer came it simply lazed there in the lows. The arches defined the 'riverness' of Clonmel town, great 'eyes' that witnessed days of leisure and livelihood, and long-gone times when horse-drawn barges brought their cargoes of coal and grain upriver from Waterford and Carrick-on-Suir, and navigated the narrow channel under the town's arch before docking at the upper quays to unload.

'Well, Huck,' Uncle Paddy turned his gaze from the bridge and grinned at his young nephew.

'Well, Uncle Paddy,' said The Boy, like a younger echo coming back. And they settled into lazy, happy silence again, punctuated by barks from Wiggles. Downriver the wrinkled lime trees at the dog track shimmered in the soft blue haze. At Dudley's Weir the supple willows and the reed beds faded into soft, transparent washes of grey green and sulphured brown. The water itself mimicked the riverbank and the sparsely-clouded sky. It was an evening of evenings, and there was music in the air. Nature's soloists arrived with some unusual instruments to hand. Impressive choristers lined the banks ready and willing to support them.

Countless little creatures left their earthy, grassy homes to join in. Clickety-clacking grasshoppers, samba rhythm damselflies, and chorus-line bumblebees took their places in the orchestra. Deep in the undergrowth, brown water rats rustled with maracas. Coots and water-hens cavorted in the reeds. Green and yellow frogs bassooned and belched. Overhead, pipistrelle bats piped their high-pitched tunes. On the mossy stones of the summer weir a pair of mating swans boogie-woogied. Farther down, on the Millrace, an otter dived for eels and splashed the water cymbals. It was a sound so pure it might have gone unnoticed, but she had rehearsed it over and over and knew when to play it for maximum effect.

'Hey, Huck!'

'What, Uncle Paddy?'

'Can you hear the elvers Presley?'

'Ha ha ha!'

The Boy couldn't contain a silvery laugh that rose and fell like a conductor's baton, damping the orchestra before bidding it soar again in a flurry of sharps and flats. Brown trout came up for flies and left winking rings on the surface. Wiggles' stubby tail went into overdrive. The magic of the evening kicked in.

Time was part of the magic. Old father time threw away his scythe and took to juggling clocks. Rain-Water, an old artist who lived at the edge of town, said that evenings like this happened because there was a studio at the outer edges of the Milky Way full of deceased artists whose job was to wash the horizon with rose madder, golden ochre and blue, till pigments streamed across the sky and flushed the evening light with colours beyond belief.

They called him 'Rain-Water' because he was always talking about Renoir, and some child mispronounced it, so now everyone took to calling him 'Rain-Water'. He was there still, dreaming of a place in the Milky Way studio, and painting the occasional canvas; filling young heads with wonderful pictures and colours. And telling tall tales that were never too tall to reach up to. The Boy succumbed to the magic of being eleven years of age, and drifted downriver in a tar-black, double-pointed, flat-bottomed boat, poled by his Uncle Paddy, with Wiggles at the bow.

Chapter 2

Wise Men, Clever Trout

The trout Paddy was stalking had tucked in behind a sally bough that had fallen into the river and was feeding confidently in the calm pool behind it. It was a difficult place to lay a dry fly accurately. If it splash-landed, it would put the fish down. If the distance were overestimated it could have snagged on the overhanging branches, spooked the fish and ruined any chance of catching it. The awkwardness of the situation was etched on Paddy's face.

He knew how clever trout were. They identify the shape and colour of insects instantly, and know the behaviour pattern of every single creature on their diet sheet. Imagine you're a trout, Paddy thought. You're in the shadowy shallows and there's an abundant hatch of insects floating on the surface above you, all behaving and appearing the same. You're enjoying the banquet. Suddenly, you notice one bug, a loner, acting out of character with the others, kicking up a hullabaloo. Wouldn't you be suspicious? I surely would, thought Paddy, coming out of his trout persona. If the fishing fly had ruffled the water, the trout would have known there was something fishy going on and ignored it.

Most rivers have scores of insects that love shimmying across the water. Caddis flies, or Sedges, zig-zag across the surface like tiny motorboats, maybe for the sheer heck of it. The females of this group, *tricoptera*, particularly enjoy skimming across the water as they deposit eggs. The equivalent of deep breathing exercises perhaps? An angler mimics their erratic behaviour by jerking the artificial fly across the surface of the water. But Caddis flies, or Water Boatmen, were not part of the trouts' menu that evening. A hatch of delicate Olive Duns was floating down and the trout were dining on them.

These tiny insects, of the order *ephemeroptera*, are very elegant creatures; the prudes of our limestone lakes and rivers. They're diminutive, slender, less than a quarter of an inch long, with abdomens like Spanish olives fluctuating between pale yellow and rich dark green.

Anglers have put some lovely names on patterns they have devised to replicate them, and The Boy knew most of them. Sometimes he'd reel-off the names to himself: the Sooty Olive, the Blue-winged Olive, the Pale Watery Dun, the Dark Emerging Olive, and Greenwell's Glory, which was devised over one hundred and twenty years ago by an Englishman, the Reverend Canon Greenwell. It's a prototype that to this day holds pride of place in every discerning fly-fisher's box. When the naturals land on the water, they extend translucent diaphanous wings upright over their bodies. They prefer to drift idly along with the flow and never get involved in the energetic, show-off tactics of their larger Caddis relatives. Perhaps at heart they are snobs rather than prudes.

Paddy poked around in the fishing bag for the battered Golden Virginia tobacco tin that masqueraded as his fly box and selected a fly called the Apple Green Dun. A good choice, he thought, to charm that finicky fish.

'That's a great auld standby when the Olives are on it, Huck,' he said, holding it against the light to inspect the hook. It had a little gold tag on the tail to imitate the egg-sack on the female and was like a twin to the real thing. 'It'll make it stand out from the crowd, if you get my drift. Stir up its curiosity, Huck. Make it look twice at the fly.'

He paused to tie the fly onto the nylon leader. 'You have to be one step ahead of them all the time,' he said, 'especially when you're after big educated trout like that one out there.'

A steely nerve, a steady hand and a keen eye were mandatory. It was essential that the fly would land three or four inches above the trout's nose, touch down softly, as a feather would on silk. Paddy was an expert. The rod swished and the line hummed through the pungent air. Every other sound was spirited away. Time was suspended: anglers, river and trout existed in a blissful bubble. Paddy raised the rod to give it the last fine-tuned flick of the wrist, then he lowered the tip towards the water in one fluid movement. The line unfurled gracefully and the reserve line coiled at his feet, sprang from the boards and out through the rod guides. It caressed the water and the fly rolled over in a lazy arc. For a split second it hovered above the water, suspended like thistle down on the air, making time and silence for itself.

The fly kissed the water directly in front of the feeding trout. It seemed that everything held its breath. Paddy stood poised. The Boy's pulse drummed in his ears. Wiggles was stock-still except for his tail which made little hints at wagging. The trout rose. His snout rippled the surface. He sucked in the Apple Green Dun. Paddy reacted. The line sprang from the water and the hook was set. The river erupted. The trout slashed the water with his tail and charged for the opposite bank, then rolled over on his side, changed direction and bolted down the river at astonishing speed. The line screamed from the reel, ripping through the water and scattering white spray into the air. A strangled squeal of excitement escaped The Boy.

'Jasus, Uncle Paddy, he's a monster.'

'After him, Huck,' Paddy roared. 'I can't turn him. I can't even slow the bugger down. I'm running out of backing line fast. Quick! Pole like hell. Push like your whole life depended on it.'

The Boy plunged the pole into the riverbed and leaned on it with every ounce of strength his eleven-year-old frame could muster. The nose of the boat turned out from the bank and he steered for the centre of the river. All of a sudden the riverbank was populated by experts.

'You're in the daddy of 'em all Paddy Whelan,' a voice roared from the riverbank.

'Watch that bank of weeds out there or you'll lose him,' someone else screamed. 'He'll bury himself in them.'

'We're watching that trout for the last six weeks, so we are. He moves in there at the same time every single evening. Half-past nine on the dot. A great timekeeper he is.'

Paddy threw his eyes to heaven and whispered over his shoulder.

'Edge up, Huck, edge up. It's The Three Wise Men, guided here by some rogue star to pester the living daylights out of us. They've come from afar to offer us their wisdom and their advice. Jasus, that's all we need now – wisdom and advice from hurlers on the ditch. Not a single one of them ever sat in a boat in their entire lives, never mind grasp a fishing rod in their hands.'

The newcomers were the Wyse brothers – all three of them retired and all dyed-in-the-wool bachelors. They had a reputation for being as nosy as vixens around a henhouse. They were the evening newspapers and the bush telegraph rolled into one. The grand masters at sourcing gossip, and the undisputed specialists at spreading it. In particular, they took endless pleasure in broadcasting the sordid details concerning the extra marital affairs of the invented upper social classes of the day, whom they referred to as 'them snobby nobs'.

Dave, Simon and James Wyse, nicknamed of course, the Three Wise Men, loved the River Suir and befriended those who loved their river also. They were neither anglers nor boatmen, yet they had a special relationship with the river. Over the years it had become part of them. They were familiar with its moods and habits and were on first-name terms with each rock on its banks. They weren't fishermen, yet they knew the good salmon lies, and places where big trout could hide.

For those willing to listen, their advice was solid and worthwhile. If a big flood came and re-charted the river, if dangerous snags got trapped on the bottom, the brothers were the first to know it and readily pass that information along. But for the moment, even Wiggles looked askance at them.

'Christ, Paddy, don't let him down over that bloody weir there or he'll make bits of you,' Dave screamed from the riverbank.

'Never mind the shaggin' weir,' James yelled. 'He's heading for that bank of weeds opposite the big chestnut. If he gets buried in them, you can whistle him goodbye.'

'Jasus Christ Almighty, Paddy, but he has a tail on him like a shovel, hasn't he Simon?'

'He has, he has,' said Simon in a sing-song voice. 'We have a great view of him from here, so we have.'

The trout turned downriver, plotting a course for the lip of Dudley's Weir, and the running commentary intensified on the bank above them. The Three Wise Men lost the run of of themselves and bombarded the boatmen with worthless advice. So excited were they, so caught up in the drama, that their counsel descended from the exalted and wise into pure gibberish. The Boy, heeding only Paddy, banked the cot sharply to run with the current and sailed at speed for the mouth of Dudley's Weir in pursuit of the trout, while the Three Wise Men trundled along the shore, trying to keep up.

The gap in the weir was a tricky place to manoeuvre safely, and often shifted character. Where the Mill Pond ended, the river divided into two diverse waterways. It was separated by an artificial island and an elongated narrow stone wall. The lethargic water on the Waterford side of the river ambled down to Dudley's Mills. The Back River they called it. A complex fusion of deep pools and narrow shallows. At one time it powered imposing mill-wheels that provided sufficient energy to sustain a thriving tanning industry.

The weir, with its narrow navigation channel, was located by the Tipperary bank of the river. Its flow was constricted between the dividing stone wall and the lofty perpendicular defence of the riverbank. The compressed water gouged its way through the narrow opening and then turned back on itself abruptly. In the process it whipped up a backwash that could dash a boat against the rocks and crush it.

'Watch that backlash there; it'll turn your nose over to the wall,' Dave warned.

'If you hit them rocks, they'll make shite of you. Won't they, Simon?'

'They will, they will,' sang Simon. 'Holy Jasus, they'll make smithereens of you, dog and all. Paddy Whelan, tell that young fella to watch out for the whirlpool or it'll suck you in and turn you arse about face.'

'Never mind that,' James shouted, 'there's a big log wedged on the bottom and if the trout wraps himself around that, you'll be shagged altogether. He'll make bits of the line, so he will.'

'Push over lad,' Simon was frothing with excitement. 'Now, young fella, now!'

The cot swung around violently and The Boy polled desperately to keep it fair. Paddy gritted his teeth and kept his eye on the taut line to the trout. Wiggles, still at the bow, barked back and forth from his front to his hind legs.

'Wiggles, you're nearly as bad as The Three Wise Men,' roared Paddy. The Wyse brothers were still going strong and their commentary looked like outlasting the trout. Now James was the lead voice.

'Ah shag it all,' he cried, 'but you were only blessed then. You only missed a big ugly rock by the skin of your teeth. Blessed, I say.'

'Is there any point in telling you any thing at all, is there? You could've been in the drink, the pair of you, and what's even worse, you could have lost the fish,' James said.

Paddy and The Boy circumnavigated the brothers' aid and brought the cot safely over the weir. Now it was tucked in under the high bank and the bow was wedged on a raft of weeds that acted as an anchor. The stern pointed downstream and avoided the grip of the robust currents. It was an ideal sanctuary. There was room to manoeuvre and Paddy had ample space to fight the fish in the mysterious waters of Dudley's Hole.

The trout fought deep and hard, bolting powerfully and stripping most of the line from the reel. It surprised them by surging to the surface without warning. It noisily thrashed about close to a nesting Pen on the far bank. The startled Pen hissed and flapped her wings, and lunged across the water towards the boat.

'Start poling Huck and get us out of here fast,' Paddy roared.

The Boy heard him, but couldn't react. He was frozen to the seat with fear. His brain said move, his body said no. The Three Wise Men came to the rescue. They jumped up and down on the bank, like dancers in a tribal ritual. They shushed and shooed frantically waving their arms all over the place. Their voodoo had the desired effect and swan withdrew to her nest.

'Thanks, men, you saved the day. That was quick thinking. Fair play to you," Paddy shouted across at the Wyse brothers, and then added, in a voice that didn't carry beyond the boat, "You can pester the living daylights out of us but you can be very useful at times like these.'

Paddy turned his full attention to the rod and line. He had somehow managed to maintain control of the trout and it was ready to be coaxed into the landing net. The Wyse brothers were off again. This time Simon led the chorus.

'For God's sake, young fella, make sure you get the net fair and square under that fish the first time round. You won't get a second shot at it. He won't, will he lads?'

'Dead right so he is. You won't get a second crack at him,' Dave replied excitedly.

'In the name of all that's good and holy,' Paddy pleaded, 'will the three of you put a bloody sock in it? You're worse than any bunch of auld women standing outside the church after a novena. Those fecking tongues of yours haven't stopped wagging since we hooked the trout.'

The trout's broad back and large tail broke the surface, two rod-lengths out from the gunnel, and they had their first opportunity to see him properly.

'Paddy, he's massive,' The Boy gasped.

'He's a damn good 'un all right. But slow down, take it easy now. He's not in the cot yet. Get the net ready and next he comes in close I'll put some pressure on and try to turn him. See if you can get the net under him then, but don't attempt to lift it till I give the word.'

'All right.'

The trout tried to make another dash but Paddy lifted the rod high over his shoulder and held back firmly. That old split cane rod was practically bent in two. The Boy thought it would snap.

'Put the net in the water now and get ready Huck. Do it very gently so as not to frighten him.' The trout came closer to the boat. Seconds passed. The Boy trembled. Paddy slid the trout in over the rim of the landing net and yelled.

'Now!'

The Boy raised the net, two-handed, the trout poured itself in over the steel hoop and the Three Wise Men erupted into applause.

'Christ, do you think we've just won the All-Ireland hurling final, or what?' Paddy said, smiling.

'That was better than any day up in Croke Park,' James Wyse said.

'And we didn't have to pay a penny to watch either,' said Dave. Paddy turned to The Boy.

'Huck was a good nickname to put on you,' he grinned. 'Sure Huckleberry Finn himself wouldn't have managed the cot better than you did this evening.'

'You're dead right there, Paddy Whelan,' chimed Simon Wyse. 'That was great manoeuvring altogether.' The Three Wise Men were belly down on the bank, their heads sticking out over the edge.

The Boy looked up at them, blushing slightly, but proud as a peacock at the way he'd handled the cot.

'Are you keeping the trout, lads?' It was almost a chorus from the three Wyses.

'It's your call, Huck,' Paddy said, turning to The Boy. 'Do you think he should swim away free, to fight another day? It's your choice now. You decide.' The Boy looked at the trout for a long moment, admiring its graceful lines. It was a magnificent specimen. A real beauty. What should he do? He looked around at the others for some hint of guidance. The Wyse brothers held their breaths, and their counsel. Paddy waited inscrutably.

'He put up a great battle, didn't he Uncle Paddy?'

'He did just that, Huck, but more, much more. He's given us the opportunity of a lifetime.'

'What do you mean?'

'Well, it's like this. On such a glorious God-given day, how many people do you think got the chance to count the spots on a five, maybe even six pound, wild brownie? Will you just feast your eyes on those colours? Those beautiful markings. The shape of him. We're really honoured and privileged, that's what we are. But as I said, Huck, it's your choice.'

The Boy gazed at the trout again. He wanted so much to keep him. The urge was so strong. But deep down, he knew he couldn't.

'The King never falls in battle, does he Uncle Paddy? I'll put him back.'

'Yippie, good on you, auld stock,' Simon clapped his hands. 'You have one great pupil there, so you have, Paddy Whelan. He'll be a good 'un yet, won't he, Dave?'

'He will, he surely will. 'Tis a right good angler he'll make.'

Paddy helped The Boy remove the fish from the net. He

wrapped it tenderly in a wet cloth, laid it on the cot's centre seat, and turned again to The Boy.

'Always handle a fish that's going back in the river with great care, Huck. Wrapped in a damp cloth, they can't struggle and hurt themselves.'

The Boy nodded. Wiggles wanted to lick the fish, his usual treat when a trout was culled for the table. But this time Paddy held him back.

'No, Wiggles, me auld pal. You can't lick this one because he's going back. You can lick the next one till he's bone dry, but not this one.' He lifted Wiggles gently and placed him at the far end of the boat. 'Now, Huck, look here carefully. The fly is caught in the top lip. Ease it out as gently as you possibly can, and then I'll tell you what to do next.'

The Boy clasped the fly between thumb and forefinger and slipped the tiny hook out without difficulty.

'Well done, Huck. That's the work of a real expert. Now, when I take the cloth away, catch him around the tail with one hand, then put your spare hand under his belly for support.'

The Boy followed Paddy's instructions to the letter. He knelt on the keel boards and leaned over the side, holding the trout with his head facing the current so he'd get a good flow through the gills.

'How'll I know when to leave him go, Uncle Paddy?'

'The trout'll tell you that. He'll let you know when he's ready.'

The Boy held the fish into the current, vaguely aware that his thumb and forefinger wouldn't meet around the girth of his tail, and watched the gill plates moving in and out as the trout soaked up oxygen from the water. Then a surge of energy pulsed through piscine muscles and with a flap of his broad tail he disappeared into the depths of Dudley's Hole, leaving The Boy with empty hands and a look of surprise on his face.

'I told you he'd let you know.' Paddy laughed heartily and wound the line back onto the reel.

They tied their cot up at the riverbank and sat on the grass opposite Clibbern Stream chatting to the Wyse brothers. The evening had already spun a mantle of light and soft shadows over the valley of the Suir. Swallows and bats skimmed low over the water, scooping up flies and moths, and rooks were settled in the chestnuts.

'Jasus, but that was tense there for a while,' James Wyse said. 'This auld heart of mine is still ticking twenty to the dozen.'

'I thought you were going to slap into the big rock when you were coming over the weir, Paddy,' Dave added, his eyes still wide with the excitement and drama of the moment. 'The tail of your cot was only inches away from it, do you know that? Only inches.'

'Sweet holy divine Dave have you no confidence at all in that young man's ability with a cot?' Paddy asked. 'Don't you know that he's the reincarnation of Huckleberry Finn, of Mississippi fame?'

'We should've guessed that,' James said.

'Did you know, young fella, that the pool where you landed that trout is one of the best places on the entire river to catch a salmon?' Simon asked, and didn't wait for an answer. 'Well it is. From the tail of the hole there right up to the lip of the weir is a great auld stand for them. Many a fine lump of a fish I saw getting caught along there.' He stretched out his arms as far as they could go, as though conjuring up a picture.

'What weight was the biggest one, Mr Wyse?'

'The biggest one ... let me think now,' he said, tugging at his ear. 'I suppose it was the one Bubbles Hanratty landed. Now that was a fine lump of a salmon, around twenty-two pounds weight I'd say. The lads and myself had to give Bubbles a hand carrying it up to the house. Isn't that a fact, lads?'

'Oh as true as we're sitting here,' James affirmed. 'We met that returned Yank on the way back up. Do you remember that, Simon? He stopped up to admire the fish. "My God is that a salmon you've got there", says he, with an accent as deep and echoey as the Grand Canyon. "It sure is", Bubbles said, and he proud as a peacock. "It's a beautiful wild Atlantic salmon and there's twenty pounds weight in him if there's a pound at all in him. It took me the best part of an hour to land him", says he. "Well, it sure is a magnificent specimen, sir. Where exactly did you capture it?" the yank asked. "I caught him in Dudley's Hole", Bubbles replied, gettin' taller by the second. "Well my good man", says the yank, "what a great relief it must be for Mr Dudley!"'

The company roared with laughter. It was an exhausting sort of laughter and it took them a while to recover from it. When they did, the conversation turned to the swan's bizarre behaviour.

'What was that all about, men?' Paddy asked, and the Three Wise men took it in turns to explain that the pen had been stoned and hassled regularly by a gang of youths out from town.

'A bunch of thugs is what they are, with nothing better to occupy their idle time and idle minds,' Dave said, adding that the Cob had been missing for several weeks and that no one knew where he was.

'It's not clear whether the same hooligans had a hand in its disappearance or not, but I'd bet a ten bob note the bastards killed it.' Simon's voice shook with a mixture of rage and pity.

'They should be stoned, not the poor innocent swans,' James said. 'Jail is too shagging good for them.'

'Now, James, I can see your point of view,' Paddy said, 'but if they're the same bunch of yobbos I think they are, then it's really their parents that I blame. I can tell you here and now that there's little or no hope of good example in their homes, I'm sorry to say. No lads – what they need is a bit of guidance and a decent education. But now, having said that, if I happened to catch them at it, I'd kick their ignorant little arses all the way up the quay. But heaven knows, we shouldn't try to judge. Like the good book says: let he who's without sin throw the first stone. Don't you agree Dave?'

'Oh, I do agree, Paddy. It's a good swift kick up the arse they need.'

And so their voices drifted away along the riverbank, out over the Suir and became part of the timelessness of the moment. On a summertime river, late in the evening, there is a period somewhere between sunset and dewfall when the line casts a long shadow across the water. It is a unique fragment of the day when receptiveness to time begins to fade; time when conversation slows down before it steals away on the breeze to rest. A time to invite in the opiates of the river.

The dense evening air collected faraway sounds and dropped them at their feet to mingle with the water timpani. The river altered its pitch and tone constantly, swerving and sidestepping, coming and going at will. The evening had surrounded them, embraced them, with a gentle hug. The intoxicated river gods had mesmerised them, and wouldn't let go. It was a magic time and a time for magic.

For four men and a boy, sitting on the banks of a river, the moment came when there was no need for words. Even the garrulous Wyse brothers yielded to the evening's soothing influence and drifted into companionable silence. Evening's ghost-grey mist slipped down from the tops of the Comeragh Mountains and along the valley floors, its roll and tumble voiceless as four men and a boy who had by chance been drawn together to witness an evening river mystery.

The last of the light outlined the soft feminine contours of Slieve na mBan and reminded them of home. Paddy turned the cot's nose out and faced it back into the flow.

'Good night,' James Wyse called, pushing through a gap in the ditch to cross over the fields for home.

'Good night men, and thanks for your company,' Paddy replied.

'Not at all, Paddy, not at all,' Dave said. 'Our thanks to you and the lad there. We haven't had such excitement in ages.'

'He was one mighty great trout, though, wasn't he young fella?' James shouted.

'One mighty great trout.' The Boy's answer came back like a wise echo. 'And he'll live to fight another day.'

The brothers' voices faded into the distance and Paddy pushed hard for the mooring under the dark shadows at Malcolmson's bounds. A corncrake persisted in the fields behind the mill. Maidenhair mist rose in patches from the river. The air and the excitement of the evening had taken their toll, and The Boy was suddenly tired.

'Huck, let's go home.'

'Is the cot tied up?'

'Tied up and secure, Captain.' Paddy touched the peak of his cap mockingly.

'All right, so,' The Boy yawned.

Chapter 3

Enter The Dalt

The swollen river was dropping back after exceptionally heavy rain. A few more dry days, Paddy Whelan thought, and it would find summer levels again, slow down, and slip back into 'old man river' mode. On the dawdling stretches, the fish, less easy to catch, would slow down. Paddy smiled wryly. When the summer lows arrived, the river joined a union and put up placards: 'go slow in progress'.

The flood gave the river a thorough cleaning – dislodged moss and dead algae and sent it on its merry way to the sea. Surging water sponged away at the scummy residues on blanket weed, and cleaned the dark lichen-topped boulders scattered throughout the river's system. The raunchy torrent gave the river an old-fashioned Saturday-night scrub-up; changed its underwear, combed its hair. Paddy patted his hairline and smiled to himself.

The Suir looked healthier. He felt it. Fish were revitalised and became more and more active as the increase in dissolved oxygen acted like a tonic in them. It had rained persistently for three days but by late morning on the fourth it had begun to ease off. By supper time it had cleared. Hazy skies and high humidity followed. Any angler worth his salt would know the advantages and take action before the river began to nap again.

It was just seven o'clock and, prior to leaving for work that morning, he awoke The Boy.

'Huck, are you awake yet?' Paddy called. 'The day's nearly over.' Still half-asleep, The Boy thought his uncle had just come in from night-fishing and wanted to show him the catch.

'Huck, are you awake yet, or gone to heaven?' The Boy was still surfacing. The voice seemed to come from far away and echo up the stairs one step at a time. The Boy sat up dreamily, then snapped awake and jumped out of bed..

'Did you get a good one? Show me,' he called out as he bounded down the stairs

'Will you stop feeding that young fella before he goes to bed,' Paddy said to Moll, who was cooking breakfast. 'It's making his brain soft, so it is.'

The Boy reached the end of the stairs and saw that his uncle had his brown shop-coat on, and a well-worn leather moneybag slung from his shoulder.

'Oh,' he gasped, as it suddenly dawned that Paddy was about to go out to work. 'I thought you had a good trout.'

'For God's sake Huck, it's only gone seven in the morning. Will you gimme a chance – the day is only a pup yet,' he said, tickling The Boy's belly-button. 'Will you go down by the Gashouse Bridge at about twelve and have a look at the river for me. If the water's dropped back a bit, and if there's a nice stain on it, tie up a few Pale Watery Duns. While you're at it, whip up three Orange Partridges as well.'

'Are we going down this evening then?'

'Easy now, easy there,' he smiled, reading the excitement in The Boy's voice. 'We'll go if the water's right – and the wind drops –

and if everything falls into place. And after I've had a bite to eat.' He paused to pat his midriff. 'I can't go down the river with an empty belly.' He smiled and tousled The Boy's hair. 'You should know that better than anyone. You're only on the river when you're after sandwiches. Heaven knows where you fit all the grub you eat. Now, make sure you put a decent bit of hackle on. I want them to float without a life belt hanging from them this time.'

'Was there something wrong with the last lot I tied up for you, Uncle Paddy?' The Boy sounded a little hurt.

'They were a bit skimpy, that's all.' Paddy looked back from the doorway. 'My auld glimmers aren't what they used to be. If the fly doesn't float high enough on the water, I can't see it. Do you know what I mean, Huck?'

'Oh, all right so, I'll put a double hackle on them. Two full feathers this time,' The Boy said irritably.

'Good man, Huck, good man. That's the spirit. By the way, there's a brown paper bag in the Sweet Afton box with a few decent feathers in it. I got them from Shuffles Brady the other night. Didn't get them for nothing, though. And I certainly didn't ask where he got the two Rhode Island roosters he had in that canvas bag of his, because I knew he'd robbed them from somewhere. Then he had the cheek to stand there with his hands hanging till I stood him the price of a pint. What's the world coming to? Is there any dacency left? Imagine that, Moll – expecting a pint for a few little feathers!'

'You were worse to take them, Paddy Whelan.' Moll was less than sympathetic. 'You knew they were stolen property.'

'He'll want a few trout as well I suppose,' Paddy went on. 'I bet he still has his First Holy Communion money. He wouldn't give you the steam off his piss.'

Moll turned from the cooker, frowning mightily.

'I didn't say piss, did I, Huck? Back me up now.' A mischievous grin creased his face.

'No, he didn't say piss. He never curses, even when he's cross,' The Boy said, backing onto the staircase to avoid the tea towel that Moll chucked at him.

'By all that's good and holy,' she said, 'I don't know which of you is worse. There's a pair of you in it, that's for sure.'

'A decent bit of hackle now,' Paddy laughed and disappeared through the doorway to avoid another flying towel.

'How many partridges did he say, Moll?'

'Three. And wash your mouth out with soap before breakfast. Do you want a rasher?'

'I'd better get dressed first.' He bounded back up the stairs. Wiggles followed at his heels and sat on the landing, raising dust with his tail.

A trip on the river was looking good. Fishing from the cot with Paddy was special, exhilarating. Their voyages always took them to different, exciting places with things to discover. The Boy looked happily at the dog.

'Hold it boy – did you hear what the man said? If everything falls into place. But don't worry your woolly head – you can come too.'

He leaned over the banister and shouted down the stairs.

'I'll have two rashers and a fried egg.'

'Go back to bed, you must be coming down with something,' Moll shouted back, her voice accompanied by the mouth-watering aroma of sizzling bacon wafting up the stairs.

The Boy made short work of breakfast and pushed the last slice of bacon between two thick chunks of bread. The scullery door, leading to the white-washed yard, was open and he could see Moll hanging out the washing. He saw the ivy on the roof of the coal shed waving about in a strong breeze, and ordered the wind to leave before the evening came.

'Strong wind is a fly-fisherman's curse. It's the bane of a dryfly man. That's what Uncle Paddy says. Do you know that, Wiggles? The bane of a dryfly man.' He handed Wiggles a crisp bacon-rind. Butter from the sandwich melted onto the floor. He reached for the latch and called back to Moll.

'I'm off to look at the river.'

'Don't be too long.'

The Boy sprang onto his bicycle and whizzed round the corner at Lil Maher's garage, almost colliding with Eily Sauvage as she stepped from the footpath.

'I'll tell Moll. You bloody little scut,' she squealed. 'You near frightened the shagging life out of me.'

'Sorry missus,' he gasped. 'I'm away down to the river in a wicked hurry.'

'Get along, you little fecker, an' slow down on that yoke.' She shook her walking cane as she spoke.

The watermark on the arches indicated that the river was fining down. Conditions were improving, looking good for the evening's fishing excursion. The Boy remembered something he often heard his uncle say.

A falling river should be fished; rising, left alone.

A heron, grey sentinel of the Suir, swooped under the bridge's middle arch and landed at the tail of the island. It stood silhouetted against the lush vegetation and its reflection stammered in the water.

'Good fishing,' The Boy yelled, and looked around to make sure no one heard him. It was half-past eight in the morning. The wind turned from the south-west into the south, and the boot-factory hooter cut the air twice. The sun made its first attempts to break through greyness. The bells of Saint Mary's began to chime.

A detour home seemed like a good idea. He pushed the bike up the steps at the bridge ending, craning to look at the scars of the mason's chisels, standing out like ancient ogham against the time-polished limestone. In a corner on the last step, a few pearls of dew glistened in a spider's web.

He pushed hard across the bridge, then eased back, free-wheeling down Raheen Road. Fog drifted up from the river and swirled around full-leaved oaks and chestnuts in the barley field. Moist foliage scattered the light, made wild patterns across the grass. Behind him, the bridge merged with the background, and across the river, the town took shape like a fragile watercolour.

Halfway down Raheen Road, he stopped and leaned his bike against the fragmented walls of a derelict house. It was once the home and place-of-work for his grandfather and great grandfather. It had been an important enough place, once. Paddy was fond of pointing it out to him on the 1832 Ordnance Survey map of Clonmel. On another map, dating from 1874, the old place is recorded as an industrial mill, and probably a blacksmith's forge not long after.

The gable-end walls stood on solid foundations that went deep into the river bed. The mill-stream, diverted from the main flow, gushed under the house through an archway in the gable. Some clever architect came up with the idea of boring a hole through the floor above – great sanitary conditions for those with nerves of steel and a steady aim.

It was one of The Boy's favourite places. Curiosity and a taste for adventure often enticed him there. Sometimes he fancied he could hear the high-pitched ring of the anvil, see the sparks flying, and his great grandfather bending over the anvil, hammering white-hot metal into shape. He pictured jennets, horses, donkeys and nags, all queued up outside waiting to be shod; and cartwheels and broken axles scattered everywhere about. He saw the flames and heard the roaring bellows, flinching a little from the loud hiss of a searing iron tempering-in the cooling cask. In its dark pungent liquid lay a legendary cure for warts. He imagined that the bright sea-laced salmon, returning to the reds, high on the river, stopped up behind the house to rest for a while; the familiar echoes from the forge, a pilot for them on their spawning journey. And he knew that, in the stillness of the night, otters came to hunt and play there, in the deep forge pool.

Opposite Lady Blessington's Weir, the bank curved into a quarter moon, as it sloped down onto sand and gravel at the water's edge. The Boy knew every watery sound and surge. Halfway along, the river rumbled over the remains of a sunken weir, and then rushed headlong into the pool behind the forge. From there it ran on through the barley field, and was finally drawn into a meeting with the main river at the point of Suir Island. Then it broke from the island's grip again, and rushed under the arches of Gashouse Bridge and on to Dudley's Mills, a mile or more below.

He came out of his reverie and was about to leave the millhouse when he spotted a salmon rising and, seconds later, a tall man scurrying along the riverbank. The Boy leaned out through a gaping hole in the wall for a better view. The fish showed silver again. A loud voice sounded above the din of the rapids. The Boy felt a surge of terror, fearing the man had fallen into the river. He scrambled higher up the wall for a better view, and saw that the man was flat on his back at the water's edge, his legs cycling the air as he struggled to hold on to his fishing rod. The fish splashed again, and the rod flexed hard into a fighting curve. The man struggled to his feet and the breeze carried his string of curses. He had hooked the salmon.

The Boy scrambled down from the wall and ran outside, gunned the imaginary twin carburettors of his Raleigh bicycle to life and hurried closer to the scene of the drama. He scaled Strand Wall and was halfway up a steep grassy embankment when the mangled strains of 'Danny Boy' rose into the morning air in short, sharp bursts. The angler's rearrangement of the original lyrics made them entirely unsuitable for public performance. It was the first time The Boy had ever felt assaulted by a song.

He watched as the angler coaxed the fish back over the crown of the hidden weir and abruptly stopped his assault on 'Danny Boy'.

'Fuck "Danny Boy", and all his relations. I have you now my auld fan-tailed darling,' the man roared, and set about impaling the plain-tive air of "Kathleen Mavourneen" on his raucous voice and dragging her, screaming, through the fresh green fields of the Old Bridge.

The Boy drew closer to the river for a better look at the angler-cum-mangler-of-songs.

'The Dalt!' he said, as the man's frame and features came clear-ly into focus. The Dalt Harrigan, celebrated angler and notorious poacher, was at that moment standing waist deep in the river and swaying at an alarming rate.

At some stage during Kathleen Mavourneen's death rattles, the salmon decided that it had had enough and bolted downriver in the general direction of Greenland. The Dalt slowly backed onto dry land and over his shoulder saw The Boy curled up on the grass convulsed with laughter.

'Hey you, over there,' he snapped, 'Get that fecking gaff.'

'It's on your back.' The Boy's answer was almost smothered by another burst of laughter. The Dalt fumbled for the shaft of the gaff.

'Be Jasus, but you're bang-on,' he snorted.

The fish was yielding to the constant rod pressure, or perhaps, the verbal abuse. It swam closer. With the salmon in calmer water, The Dalt's confidence grew. He wedged the butt of the rod against his thigh and reached into his jacket pocket. He snatched a bottle of whiskey and put it to his lips. It was then it dawned on The Boy that the angler was pickled to the gills; drunk as any lord. He staggered violently as he slipped the gaff over his shoulder and threw it towards The Boy.

'Grab that, young fella, and when I tell you, give it to me. Do you hear me now?' The Boy nodded and picked it up. The Dalt intensified his battle with the fish. The whiskey coursing through him gave him energy. But like the salmon, deep down, he was weary.

'Gimme that yoke,' he croaked.

The Boy handed him the gaff. Across the river, a pair of water hens chased each other in and out through the reed beds, part of that age-old ritual. On the rusting roof of a boat shed, two grey crows squabbled over a morsel of food. The ancient salmon rolled over on its side for the last time. With one fluid movement of The Dalt's gaff, it arched under its point. The fish landed at The Boy's feet.

The Dalt delivered the final blow, then the energy drained from him and he sagged to the ground, sweat streaming down his face. He reached into his jacket and drank again from the whiskey bottle. Red-eyed, he looked up at The Boy and it was a long time before he spoke.

'Good on ya young fella. If you were big enough I'd stand you a pint. And before I forget, tell that uncle of yours I'll learn him how to fish.'

He never did.

Chapter 4

Eel Fares the Land ...

There was great trout fishing after the flood. The weather was unsettled and rain every other day kept the river high and held that tea-brown stain beloved of dryfly anglers. Paddy and The Boy were on the river at every opportunity and the Suir was bounteous.

'If eating trout made the neighbours wise,' Paddy said, 'we'd be living in the midst of geniuses.' They fished and fished until the weather moved from days of rain to weeks of continuous sunshine, and when the vibrant, brown trouty waters tired and the river dozed again, The Boy turned his attention to eel fishing. It was the poor relation of fly-fishing but he liked it well enough and it kept him out of trouble. That summer he caught enough eels to fill barrels. One was almost five pounds weight, as thick as the tube in a bicycle-tyre, and it had skin like ebony. But it was the eel he caught one Saturday morning at Burke's Bacon Factory that he remembered best.

Aggie Flannery, who lived around the corner, loved eels.

'I'd ate 'em for breakfast dinner and supper,' she said. Fibber Fogarty had an endless craving for them.

'The only way to cook them,' Peadar Strappe declared, 'is in the company of a few rashers. But don't look away from the frying-pan, or the eels might scoff the rashers while your back is turned!'

Not everyone in the neighbourhood liked eels. Maggie down-the-street hated them so much she could scarcely bring herself to say the word. Miss Morris, though, was more eloquent in her distaste for them.

'Those dirty rotten yokes are the creation of the devil himself,' she said. The very mention of eels was enough to drive girls away, screaming. Knowledge like that was a powerful weapon for a boy to have, and it was often used to discourage girls who insisted on joining in the boys' games.

'Yes we *are* playing cowboys with you.'

'No you're not. Girls don't play cowboys.'

'Yes they do.'

'No they don't. There's no such thing as girl cowboys.'

'There is so.'

'There is not.'

'We'll stick a big, long, slithery, black eel down inside yer knickers then.' That was enough to start the screams and the retreat.

The paraphernalia required for bobb fishing was simple enough: a bamboo cane, a length of string tied to the top of the cane, and dozens of earthworms. Stitched together, with fine cotton thread, the ball of worms was the essential tool for catching eels. The bobb was the business end of fishing tackle.

The Boy took pride in the size and the quality of the bobbs he made. The larger and squishier they were, the better he regarded them and he'd sit for hours once a week on the doorstep sewing worms together. But no matter how well it was done, by the end of a week's eel-fishing, the bobb looked a horrid sight and reeked to high heaven.

One morning, Aggie Flannery beckoned him from across the street. She was standing by the door with a sweeping brush in hand.

'Will you hold that shovel under the dirt for me?' she asked. 'The back is killing me. Can't bend down. I see you're going down fishing.'

'I am.'

'Will you bring me back a few eels. I didn't get any from you in a long time.'

'It's hard to keep everyone happy, Missus Flannery,' The Boy said. 'Fibber gives me a bar of chocolate for 'em.'

'Well, if you bring them back to me, I'll give you two bars of chocolate. How's that?'

'That's a deal. I'll get you a bucketful of them.' On the way to the river, he called in to Fibber Fogarty and told him that Aggie Flannery had offered him two bars of chocolate to give her his catch of eels.

'Is that right now?' asked Fibber. 'Well, I'll give you the same, and twopence as well, if you bring the eels to me.'

'Deal,' The Boy said.

There were several first-class places on the river where a boy running such a profitable eel business could go. Top of his list was the Old Quay, outside Burke's Bacon Factory. On slaughter days, the discharge of blood and guts from the plant attracted hundreds of eels.

The retail end of the bacon business was on O'Connell Street in Clonmel, where they sold rashers, sausages, pigs' heads, crubeens, skirts, kidneys and slabs of bacon. The butchers were often annoyed by whipper-snappers shouting in through the shop doorway. The mock-request was always the same:

'My mother said you're to give me a pig's head, and you're to leave the two eyes in it so it'll see us through the week.'

'Will I cut the tongue out,' one butcher invariably retorted, 'the same as I'm going to do with yours?'

The slaughter facilities were on the quay behind the bacon shop, and were accessed via a narrow, busy thoroughfare. The Boy settled down with his bamboo pole and ball of worms on the quay fronting the slaughter house. This is the place to be, he told himself, to catch a bag of eels. He was as expert as anyone in the art of eel-fishing. Bobb-fishing, unlike other forms of angling, did not require a fishing hook. But when a bite registered, it was essential to heave on the pole immediately in order to wedge the sewing thread between the eel's fine teeth. Simple but effective.

The eels began to nibble at the bobb almost immediately. In less than an hour, a dozen or more were wriggling in his bag. The road was busy that day, with trailers full of pigs arriving for slaughter. The trucks and tractors lined both sides of the road and the breeders stood around smoking and chatting or walking from one trailer to the next, admiring each other's stock. Now and then a few farmers would slip up the lane beside the factory. When they returned, their mouths were porter-stained. The pigs created a desperate racket, squealing and squawking constantly. They urinated and defecated endlessly. Men in white overalls came and power-hosed the mess straight into the river.

For a while, the eels lost interest in the bobb, and The Boy sat down on the limestone kerbs, his legs dangling over the quay wall, and his back relaxed against the railings. Parties of well-dressed, cheerful people passed by intermittently. One man with a bright-red face and a dark suit looked trapped inside his shirt and tie, and poked a finger between his neck and collar to ease the pressure. The

women were brightly dressed. Some tweed-suited madams balanced precariously on stiletto-heeled shoes as they side stepped pig-
shit. Others wore dresses with large flowery patterns. Walking gardens, The Boy mused. Most of the ladies wore big extravagant hats
and one wore a bonnet festooned with colourful, exotic feathers.

'Uncle Paddy could make wonderful trout flies if he had that,'
The Boy thought.

He was so taken by the parade that he forgot about the bobb
dangling in the river. He was reminded of it quite suddenly by a
strong tug on the line and instinctively whipped the bamboo over
his shoulder, but with far too much force. The eel rocketed from
the water and sailed through the air overhead. In mid-flight, it part-
ed company with the bobb and the worms snapped from the
string. Before he could shout a warning, the squirming serpent
wrapped itself around the feathery hat, and its tail end wriggled and
slithered about the woman's nose and spectacles.

Mayhem accompanied the reeking, unravelling ball of worms
as it landed directly on her bosom. They slithered down her apple-
blossom dress. One of the party tried to beat the eel to death with
an umbrella. Another attempted to banish the dead worms with
several blows of her black leatherette handbag. The woman in the
feathery bonnet stood with hands and arms outstretched. Her eyes
were wide and screaming, but no sound escaped her open mouth,
and she was paler than the marble on any town statue.

The rest of her companions screamed their heads off. One irate
gentleman ran towards The Boy with his fists in the air. The erst-
while bobb-fisher darted under the railings, ran along the street and
escaped across the Old Bridge. The man was soon outpaced by
young, faster limbs, gave up the chase, and had to settle for shouts
and fist-shaking at The Boy's retreating figure.

'Look at the state you have my mother in, you little gutter-snipe,' he roared. 'How in God's name is she going to attend a wedding now? Just look at the state of her.'

The Boy waited till the coast was clear, then made his way home via Fibber's workshop. He entered with a bag of eels and came out with two bars of chocolate and two pennies to jingle. Next stop was Aggie Flannery's.

'You'll never guess what happened today Aggie,' he said, handing her a bag of eels, purloined from Fibber's bag.

Chapter 5

The Pig Takes Flight

The old warehouses along the quay were in bad shape. They had lain idle since the turn of the twentieth century, when barges ceased to trade on the river. The roofs had caved in and masonry peeled from the walls. It was not a pretty picture.

Burke's premises marked a gory confluence. The town sewage joined forces with the blood-and-guts from the factory. It was a smelly place but The Boy found it exciting to be there. The day the pig escaped, that was one of the best. It began with a shout.

'Grab that pig, Tom! Grabbim, for fuck's sake!'

'I can't get near him, Murt. He's too shagging nippy for me. As quick as your sister Mary is any day, if not faster.'

'Mind your mouth, Tom. Grab that pig or we'll be sacked.'

'Are ya thick, as well as stupid Murt?' Tom roared. 'Can't you see I can't get near the bastard – he's way too fast for me.'

The pig was making one final, desperate bid to escape the butcher's knife. One moment, it looked like Tom was chasing the pig, then it seemed the pig was chasing Tom. Some factory workers across the street, stood leaning against a wall, watching the drama unfold, but they refused to help.

'Fair play Tom, but you'd want to give up the drink for a bit if you want to catch that little porker. He looks an awful lot fitter than you do,' one of them jeered.

'Far trimmer too,' added another. Tom managed to get a fleeting grip on it by the ear, but it ran between his legs and knocked him flat. The crowd roared with laughter. It was too much for Tom. He raised one finger in the air, walked up the street, and disappeared into the pub on the corner of Bridge Street.

Another boy, Jimmy Rankin, arrived to fish for eels too, but changed his mind when told what was happening.

'Come on quick,' he said, 'there's a few bob to be made from this, if we play our cards right.' The two boys stood their rods against the railings and ran to join the men who had taken over the chase from Tom.

'We want to help you catch the pig,' Jimmy said.

'Fair play,' one of the men said. 'Run down there and stand between the railings and the goods store. For Christ's sake, whatever you do, don't let that thick bastard of a pig get past you.' The two boys moved into position, spread their legs apart, and waved their arms about like absurd puppets.

'Watch out there, Mister. He's coming around the side of the lorry,' Jimmy yelled.

'What shagging side is that?' shrieked the man.

'Well, he was at the front side mister, but he went up the street again while you were shouting at us,' Jimmy laughed.

'It's not funny at all, young fella. That animal is worth a lot of money. Pig meat is a valuable commodity.'

'We'll see some of that money so, won't we mister, because we're helping you catch him?'

'I'll give you thruppence each, if you do what you're told.'

'Sixpence,' yelled Jimmy.

'I'll give you a good boot in the arse.'

'Four pence each and you have a deal mister.'

'Done.'

One of the white-coat supervisors stood on the steps. He held a gadget by his side shaped like an electric razor. Jimmy said it was a zapper for prodding the pigs into submission. His father worked in the factory and that's how he knew about it. It was an electric stunner with two prongs at one end, and it worked on batteries.

'When they poke the pig's arse with it the electricity stings the shite out of them. The beasts do what they're told then,' Jimmy said. 'My Dad has one rigged up at home to keep cats and dogs out of the garden. Ma hates them piddling all over her roses.'

'Ah Jimmy,' The Boy said, 'by the time your mother gets into the garden any self respecting cat or dog would be long gone. How could she give them a dag of it then?'

'You have me all wrong friend. It works like this. Dad has a wire set up that's running around the edge a the garden. The wire is connected to the zapper, inside the kitchen window. The gadget itself is hooked up to a twelve-volt tractor battery on the windowsill. When Ma sees an animal coming through the hedge, she pushes the gadget down onto two pennies soldered to the wires coming from the battery. See what I mean?'

'Not really, Jimmy.'

'Well listen then. This is the best bit. When the prongs on the zapper make contact with the pennies, an electric shock runs down along the wire, and Zap! Zing! there goes another dog or cat never to be seen again. Great, isn't it?'

'Jasus,' The Boy gasped, 'I'm glad none of our pets live up your way or they'd come home frizzled up like a rasher. Anyway, if your father knows so much about that yoke why isn't he running around with it helping the men trying to catch that pig?'

'Because he's the foreman and wears the white coat. He gives the orders to a bloke, who tells another sham to give the orders to the fellas chasing the pig. Do you get me?'

'Holy Divine, Jimmy. He must be raking in the money having a big job like that.'

'Well, it's like this. He never goes to work on Mondays and on certain Fridays he only goes in to collect the wages. Then, he goes up town to the pubs and bookies. Oh, it's a great job all right, but he never gives me money out of the wages 'cause the bollox never has any left.'

While Jimmy was talking about his father, two more pigs jumped bail. One was an enormous fat sow, black with the dirt. She was far slower than the other fugitives. The men caught up with her and dragged her squealing through the factory gates. Her tail was barely out of picture when a large boar turned down the street and came directly for the two boys.

The designated zapper man lunged at it but he missed. Then he panicked.

'Don't let that fat bastard get past you, lads, whatever happens. I want the privilege of slitting its throat myself. Watch out he doesn't get inside you. He might fall into the river.'

'Don't fuss, Mister. We'll turn him back. No worries,' Jimmy said. They spread their legs again, waved their arms about, and roared as loud as they possibly could, but the boar kept on coming.

'Shout louder Jimmy! Imagine we're at a hurlin' match.'

'Me lungs are bursting, Quigs. I can't.'

The boar grew larger with every yard it gained and it had a vicious look in its eyes.

'Don't let 'im past you, for Gods sake lads,' the man in the white coat pleaded. The Boy's legs felt weak and his companion had turned an even more ghastly shade of pale than the woman with the feathery bonnet and the live eel.

'Holy shit Jimmy,' he croaked. 'Look at the size of him. He's like an elephant.'

'He's bigger than a rhino, Quigs.' Jimmy's voice quivered with fear. 'Shag this for a game. I'm out of here. Raise the white flag or be trampled to death.'

The boys turned and ran for their lives down the quay with the pig hot on their heels.

'Shagging cowards! Yellow-bellies, the pair of you. Neither of you could capture a weak fart under the blankets.'

When they reached the end of Old Quay, lady luck smiled on them. Instead of running on down the quays, the pig did a u-turn at Power's Warehouse onto Quay Street. It was heading back into the arms of the capture squad. They seized their opportunity and ran back after it, screaming as loud as they could.

'Get up there, you big fat salty rasher,' Jimmy yelled after it. Another runaway was dragged through the gates as they neared the factory, its squeals sharp enough to cut through solid steel. The Boy swore to himself that he'd never eat another rasher sandwich.

The squad tried to catch the pig. It side stepped and ran up Blue Anchor Lane. It was heading for the main street.

'Get after it fast, lads,' the zapper man ordered.

'How much will ya give us for catching it again Mister?' The Boy asked.

'What do you mean? – you didn't do anything at all yet.'

'Yes, we did Mister,' Jimmy said. 'We fooled that pig into think-ing it was hunting us. We tricked it back up the street. It was you that let him escape, not us.'

'Jasus, there's no doubt Rankin, you're going to make one mighty great con artist. There's no doubt whatsoever in me mind about that. An extortionist, that's what you are. I'll give you six-pence each, and that's my final offer.'

'What's an extortionist?' Jimmy asked, as they ran up Blue Anchor Lane.

'I'm not sure Jimmy,' The Boy said. 'I think it's a bloke who works in a circus.'

'What? Is that fat bastard calling me a clown?'

When they got to O'Connell Street they heard people scream-ing in Lamb's drapery shop and crossed the street to check it out. It was Mr Lamb himself.

'Get out! Get out of here,' he screamed. 'I don't want pigs in my shop.'

'Does he mean us?' said Jimmy .

'Of course he doesn't, you ninny-hammer. He's hopping mad because the pig left a big plomper on the floor. I saw a customer scraping his shoe on the step.'

'Ha ha ha. His pig skin shoes are pig-shite-shoes now.'

The pig bolted out the drapery door and up the street and they followed it.

'Don't let it get past you this time lads,' the capture squad pleaded.

'Jasus, we can't run away again, do you hear me Jimmy?' The Boy said. 'We'll lose face entirely if we scamper.'

The pig had only one escape route. It turned down the lane., but the zapper man was waiting at the other end, ready to sting the pig into submission. He struck, but his aim wasn't good, and he zapped the swine on the snout instead of the rump. It jumped three feet in the air and when it touched down again it bolted straight across the road, under the railings, and into the river.

'I never knew pigs could swim, Jimmy.'

'Didn't know they could fly either.'

'But they can't fly, Jimmy.'

'That one made a mighty good attempt at it'

The factory hands were taking bets on whether or not the pig would reach the safety of the island. Jimmy's father offered 20/1 that it would. After securing the bets he nudged his way through the crowd and joined them at the railings.

'One of the men said you were helping to catch the beast,' he said.

'We were, and doing very well at it too, till your man there gave it a dunt in the snout with the zapper and drove the pig stone mad and then it ran straight across the road and flew straight inta the river,' Jimmy said, without taking a breath.

'Pigs can't fly son.'

'Would you like to bet on it, Dad?'

The beast attempted to swim against the current but it tired and turned downriver again. Several women crossed over from the bacon factory, their white overalls and net caps stained with pigs' blood. The scabbards slung around their waists held two knives.

'Holy Christ, Betty,' a tall, thin woman shouted gruffly, 'will you look at that big fat pig swimming out there in the river?'

'The cheek of you, Nellie Flynn! How dare you refer to my husband in such a manner!' Betty's rosy cheeks wobbled and her voice full of fun. 'He's a great deal more than a big fat pig. He's a gigantic, lazy, good-for-nothing pig, and nothing less.'

'Well, at least that pig is a lot cleaner than the swine I have at home, Betty,' Nellie said.

'Oh, I'd love to be married to a dirty old man,' one of the younger women said, reaching for the man beside her.

'You're disgusting, Gertie,' he said, grabbing her around the waist.

'Ah, seriously girls,' Nellie continued, 'my fella is grand and cuddly, only he grunts a lot.'

'My hubby has three distinctive grunts.' Betty's eyes sparkled with mischief. 'One is a short sharp grunt when he wants the feeding trough topped up. Then he has a double snort grunt, which means he's off down to the pub and I won't see him again till the early hours of the morning. And as for any other kind of grunting that he does, well, really and truly girls, that's none of your shagging business.' The women fell over themselves laughing. They slapped each other on the shoulders and pulled out handkerchiefs to wipe away the tears.

'Aren't pigs wicked stupid animals all the same?' one of of the younger women whispered in The Boy's ear.

'Why do you say that, miss?'

'Well, it's like this. If I was that pig, which of course I'm not, I'd just let meself drown out there so I would.'

'Why, miss?'

'Well, it'd be a much better way to go than having your throat slit from ear to ear while you're still alive, wouldn't it? And then after the shock of having your throat cut, the buggers hang you upside-down on a big hook and let the blood drain out of your body. Drip, drip, drip, till your dead as a fucking pig. Shag that for a way to kick the bucket. Just give me a nice cosy river to drown in any day of the week.'

'I see what ya mean all right,' The Boy said, shivering at the very thought of either option. Jimmy's father roared from across the street at the women.

'Get back inside now, this minute, you have the whole production line held up in there. You're entitled to a ten-minute break, not a day's holiday.'

'Ah go on, Mr Rankin. Be a little dote, won't you? We're way ahead on production today, so we are, and we're having great gas. Won't you give us just another few minutes, please sir?' Nellie put on her best pleading voice.

'Inside this minute, or I'll dock pay for every second that you're late, so I will.' Rankin growled. 'And that goes for each and every one of you.'

'That bastard wins the gold medal for prize pig of the year,' Nellie muttered viciously as they trooped back in through the factory gate.

'You're an awful case altogether, Nellie Flynn,' Betty said, shaking her head.

The pig made several unsuccessful attempts to climb onto a small island before it eventually found its footing and clambered ashore to run into the dense undergrowth. The men gathered around Rankin to figure out the best way to recover the beast.

'How in Christ's name are we going to get over this one?' said Rankin.

'One of us could swim over there, tie a rope around him and then drag him back?' Noel Dalton suggested.

'Very clever, very clever altogether, Noel,' said Rankin. 'But will you tell me this – how long are you working in that pig factory?'

'Fifteen years or more, I suppose.'

'And what do you do in there day after day? Can you tell me that, Noel?'

'What kind of a dopey question is that to ask? You're the main ganger,' Noel snapped at Rankin. 'You know exactly what I do in there. I slaughter the pigs – slit their pink little throats, that's what I do.'

'Well then, apart from killing them what other purpose does slitting their throats serve Noel?'

'Jasus, what's this? The inquisition all over again, is it?'

'No, it's not, Mr Dalton. I was just trying to establish how in Christ's name you intended to bleed down a fucking drowned pig, that's all.'

'Oh very smart indeed boss.' Noel grinned from ear to ear. 'But as you're so shagging clever, you figure out what were supposed to do.'

'We'll get a loan of Paddy Whelan's cot Noel – that's what we'll do. Then we can ferry the pig back over here while he's still alive and worth a few bob,' Rankin said, applying the coup de grâce. He turned and shouted to The Boy.

'Hey, young fella! Run up to the bakery and ask your uncle Paddy if I can borrow the cot. Tell him what's after happening and that I have to ferry that valuable pig off the island. And tell him that I'll look after him for doing me the favour.'

'I don't think he'll be at the bakery now, Mr Rankin,' The Boy said, 'but I'll run up to see anyway.' He cut off to the bakery but soon came back.

'The woman at the bakery said that Uncle Paddy's out on delivery and won't be back.'

'Tear up home so, and ask Moll if can I borrow the cot for a couple of hours. Tell her that Tom Kennedy is going to pole it for me. He goes fishing with Paddy sometimes so she won't mind giving us the loan of it once she knows that he's going to be in the pilot's seat.'

'Where is Tom, by the way?' Rankin inquired.

'The last time I saw him, he was being chased all over the street by that pig,' someone quipped.

'He's gone for a packet of fags,' someone else said, by way of a smokescreen, for Tom was by then comfortably entrenched in the pub.

Chapter 6

Operation Curly Wee

Moll took the keys of the cot down from their hook on the dresser, and handed them to The Boy with a thoughtful expression on her face.

'Tell Tony Rankin that he must finish with that cot before seven. Paddy said to me this morning that you were going down for a few casts after tea.'

'I will.'

'Don't take anyone down to the mooring with you when you go to bring up the cot. We don't want people to know where the pole and paddles are hidden.'

'I won't.'

'Be careful poling her up, won't you?'

'I will.'

'And you're not, under any circumstances, to go with them to rescue that pig. It'll be too dangerous with an unpredictable animal aboard.'

'Aw, Moll, I'll be grand.'

'No, you won't be grand. And that's my last word on it.' She wagged her finger till it almost touched his nose. 'Mind what I said, now,' she called after him as he rushed through the doorway.

Rankin and the others were leaning on the railings when he got back with the keys.

'Moll said that you can borrow the cot, Mr Rankin, but only if you swear to agree with a few conditions.' The Boy spoke with what he hoped was authority in his voice.

'And what would they be, lad?'

'The cot must be back at the mooring before seven. Uncle Paddy and me are going fishing.'

'Done,' said Rankin.

'It's my job to get the cot and bring it back down again, and that's because we don't want anyone to know where the pole and paddles are kept. And she says that I'm not allowed out in the cot while you're carrying that pig, just in case he capsizes it and we all get drowned.'

'Agreed,' said Rankin.

The Boy poled the cot up, a following breeze helping him keep her nose to the current. There was very little water under the small arch at the Gashouse Bridge, not enough to get under it without scraping the bottom. He took it under the town arch instead where the currents were strong, but fairly predictable, and steered as close as he could to the quay wall, poling hard to pick up speed. He was surprised by how quickly the nose cut through the water and glided under the arch. In the wink of a bridge's eye, he was safely on the other side. The pole disturbed a lamprey eel. It swam away and startled a pair of salmon out into the centre of the river. The lamprey-and-salmon moment transported him to a different world and it took him three-quarters of an hour to get from the mooring up to the rendezvous with Rankin.

'What took you so long?'

'I got here as fast as I could. When I was passing the tail of the island I saw that pig. He's in the middle of a load of brambles and bushes.'

'Are you sure?' he asked. The Boy nodded. Rankin threw his eyes to Heaven and started swearing. The Boy paddled over to the quay wall, tied up, then climbed up the steel ladder and stepped onto the road.

'Thanks young fella,' Rankin said, and slipped some coins into his hand. When he counted them he had four shillings and six-pence.

'Look what your father gave me for bringing up the cot Jimmy.'

'Jasus, that's more than he gives me in a year.' Jimmy looked across at his father, who was now pacing up and down trying to find Tom. He was very agitated.

'Where the hell is Tom Kennedy?' he roared. 'He's never around when I want him?'

'I'm right here,' Tom said, and casually leaned up against the railings beside the boys.

'I don't have to ask what you were doing – you have a grin like a Cheshire cat all over your face,' said Rankin. 'Are you in a fit state to pole the cot, so we can get the pig off that island?'

'I didn't hear any one asking me officially to do that particular job.' Tom sounded indignant. 'Nor did I hear what I was going to get paid for it either.'

'Well, if you were here I'd have asked you,' Rankin snorted. 'And you needn't worry – I'll see to it that you get a just reward.'

'I'll need another good cot-man to do the job with me,' pursued Tom. 'The Dalt might do it if he's not too busy and the price is right.'

'Christ Almighty,' groaned Rankin. 'Do you want to break us or what?'

'You'd swear the money was coming out of your own pocket, Rankin.'

'It might be a hell of a lot cheaper for the company if I left that pig over there altogether instead of paying half the fecking town to get it back.'

'Half the town? Now that's a bit of an exaggeration, boss. But please yourself,' Tom smirked, knowing he had Rankin in a stranglehold.

'Oh all right then. Get whoever you want, but get the job done before six – the young lad there must have the cot back at the mooring before seven.' Tom leaned over and tapped The Boy on the shoulder, then whispered in his ear.

'You're the only one I can trust here,' he said in a conspiratorial tone. 'Now, dag up to the pub, will you, and slip in the side door so that Rankin won't see you going in. The Dalt is in there having a few pints. Tell him I said that it's all systems go. The two of you wait there for about fifteen minutes and then get down here. In the meantime, I'll tell Rankin that you've gone over to the house looking for him. Quick, now, and I'll see you right for money.'

The Dalt looked up as The Boy entered. He was sitting at the far end of the bar, and had just taken possession of a pint of creamy stout.

'Well me auld stock, and how's the second-best cot-man in the world? The Three Wise Men told me that you took the cot down over Dudley's weir after a big trout all on your own.'

'I did and I didn't,' The Boy said. 'Uncle Paddy told me what to do.'

'Ah now, you're far too modest altogether. As far as I'm concerned, you're still the second best cot-man in the whole wide world.'

'I suppose you're the best?'

'Indeed I am not,' he laughed. 'Paddy Whelan is the best man there is. But mind you though, it was myself that learned him.'

'Tom said to tell you it's all systems go. He told me to sneak in through the side door so that Mr Rankin wouldn't see me. Why?'

'Why what?' said the Dalt.

'Why didn't Tom want Mr Rankin to know that I was coming here to get you?'

'Oh, don't you worry your little head about that now, laddie,' said The Dalt. 'Just make sure you say nothing to anybody about it. This little matter is adult business, between Tom and me and no one else.' He caught The Boy's arm roughly and squeezed a thruppenny bit into his hand.

'That's the price of your silence. Away down with you now and I'll follow shortly.'

Back on the quay, preparations were well under way to recapture the pig and Tom Kennedy was singing merrily.

And as we sail around Cape Horn, heave away, haul away,
You'll wish to God ya never were born, we're bound for South
Australia.
Haul away o rollin' king, heave away, haul away,
Haul away o hear me sing, we're bound for South Australia.

'Blimey mate, anyone'd fink you wuz sailin' to the far reaches o' the earf.' The voice belonged to a young man in the crowd. 'Just as easy to sling a ruddy 'ook over on that there island, mate, and lasso the poor fing.'

'Well, if it's not Patrick Ryan, the first and only son of James Ryan that's married to Kitty Butler that I went to primary school with,' Tom said, with withering sarcasm. 'When did you get back home from the big smoke of London young fella?'

'Free days ago, guv. But the name's Michael, mate, not young fella.'

'There you go again, calling me quare names. For your information, mate is what I eat with cabbage and spuds, and I haven't a clue what a guv is. Call that pig over there mate if you want to. But rest assured, there's no returned Irish cockney going to call me mate, or guv either.' Tom Kennedy looked and sounded agitated. 'How long are you over there in blighty – can you tell me that?'

'I've been over nearly six mumfs now mate – sorry, I mean sir.'

'Well, you should be ashamed of yourself, so you should, coming back here after six months with an English accent on you as thick as the fog on the Thames in the depths of winter. And look at the state of you. Winkle-picker shoes, drain pipe trousers and hair with so much grease in it you could start yer own shagging oil company. Did you know that I worked in England for seven long years?'

'No guv. Sorry – sir, I mean.'

'Well I did, but I never lost me own identity while I was over there. When I speak a foreign language like English at least I speak it with an Irish brogue. And what's more, I wouldn't be using it at all only for the shagging British kicked the shite out of this little nation of ours till we stopped speaking our native Gaelic.' He paused to catch his breath before continuing. 'Well, nearly stopped anyway because it isn't lost entirely yet. And that's because in the long run we succeeded in knocking enough crap out of them to make them realise that they couldn't mess around with the Irish. Oh yeah, they got the message all right, and eventually they pissed off back to where they came from. Well, most of them anyway. And then, after such a mighty struggle on your behalf mind, you go over there for little more than a wet week and come back here with a cockney accent that could be cut in two.'

'I see what you mean mate. Sir, I mean.'

'Fair play to you, young fella you're getting the hang of it already. Now listen to what I have to say to you because this is for your own good, so it is. When you go back over there hold your head up high and talk like an Irishman. You'll feel a hell of a lot better for it,' Tom said, feeling much better himself.

'Jasus Tom, but you're one cantankerous bugger, do you know that?' The Dalt had just arrived from the pub. 'I thought it was Theobald Wolfe Tone himself that I was listening to for a minute.'

'Right, let's get on with this fecking job,' said Kennedy, changing tack.

The preparations to rescue the islanded pig got under way in earnest. Rankin was doing the job that he did best and passed orders on to others. The Dalt and Tom Kennedy issued orders left right and centre. They had people racing in every direction, fetching and carrying for them. For thirty-five minutes there was frantic activity on the quayside. Rankin looked very officious as he stood beside the railings with a clipboard, ticking-off the goods as they were handed down into the boat. The Dalt stopped for a moment.

'Every mission worth its salt should have a code-name,' he announced. 'And this mission of ours should be called "Operation Curly Wee".' There were nods and mutters of approval from everyone except Rankin, whose attention was glued to the contents of his clipboard. The Dalt insisted on giving a detailed description of each item before he lowered it down to Tom Kennedy. Slightly tipsy, they began to enjoy the task in hand, much to Rankin's annoyance.

'One rope coming down, Tom.'

'Check!' said Rankin, officiously.

'Slightly frayed at one end,' The Dalt added.

'What end would that be, sir?' Tom said, saluting The Dalt.

'The beginning end, you dunderhead! What kind of a ship's stores officer are you at all?'

'The thick kind, sir.'

'One electric battery-charged zapper coming down.'

'Check!'

'With enough zip to zap the arse off the most stubborn pig, English or Irish,' said The Dalt. It was too much for Rankin.

'Cut out that messing about, the pair of you,' he growled.

'Yes, sir,' they said in unison, and saluted Rankin.

'Four pieces of thin rope, each one of them the same length coming down as one single rope,' sang The Dalt.

'You dirty eejits,' said Rankin.

'Correction,' said The Dalt. 'Three pieces of thin rope coming down, one piece of thin rope floating off down the river.'

'Two long sticks. One enamel basin, five large loaves, a half bag of maze and a partridge in a pear tree,' Tom Kennedy sang and laughed.

'Two large bottles of water comin' down,' The Dalt grinned. 'Don't drop them whatever you do, Tom.'

'The river water's not good enough for you, then?' queried Rankin.

'You wouldn't expect us to drink the water out of that river would you, boss?' asked Tom.

'Sure I told one of the lads to go and get you a few large bottles of stout just in case you get thirsty.'

'God bless you, boss.' said The Dalt. 'Catching a pig can be wicked thirsty work.' Someone handed him a sack..

'One sack coming down, Tom, with this and that inside – several large bottles of creamy stout included.'

'I have it, Dalt, safe and sound.'

'Check,' Rankin said, officious again.

'That seems to be the lot,' said The Dalt.

'Jasus, it'd want to be,' commented Rankin. 'For a while there I was convinced you were heading for South Australia.'

'When a pig gets away from the herd like that boss, and when it's out in the bush alone, it regains some of the characteristics of the wild boar, and it could take us ages to catch him again,' grinned The Dalt. 'As a matter of fact, we could be out there all night trying to put manners on him.'

'You'd better have that cot back here by six or half past at the latest,' The Boy said, with intent.

'Don't worry young fella. I was only joking there. We'll be back.'

The cot swung around the head of the island and out of sight behind the trees. 'Operation Curly Wee' had begun. The Boy grinned and stuck his thumb in the air.

'Go on home now, the lot of you.' Rankin turned his attention to the spectators. 'The show's over.'

But it wasn't: it was just beginning.

The rescue team carried the equipment onto the island and sat on a fallen bough to organise the campaign. The island was long and narrow, covered in tall trees and dense undergrowth. Most trees there were alders, and there were some beeches. They'd grown from seeds that came down with floodwaters over many years. When the seeds sprouted they made a claim on the land. As the island matured it nursed its own seeds and saplings and it became self-sufficient. It was a haven for wild life: a home to mallard, swans, piebald coots, water hens, rats, mice and a myriad of songbirds. Two pairs of breeding otters lived there too. For the duration of 'Operation Curly Wee' the residents had no choice but to share their domain with a pig and two tricksters.

'So that's the plan then, is it?' asked The Dalt.

'I reckon that's the best way to do it anyway,' replied Tom.

'Right then. We'll have a quick swig before we head off into the deepest heart of the jungle.'

'Good idea, Dalt. Give us one of them stout bottles from that sack there.'

'Naw, not that stuff, Tom. Grab a bottle of the "holy water".' Tom handed him the bottle and Dalt uncorked it, threw his head back and closed his eyes.

'Holy fuck, there's some kick in that stuff,' The Dalt gasped. 'Where did you get hold of such a grand drop of the Mountain Dew?'

'Never mind where I got it – just give me a sup before you guzzle the lot. You have a mouth like a gully trap, so you have. Steady on. Don't you know we need some of it for that pig as well?' Between them, they emptied one of the bottles of poteen, and felt in fine fettle as they began their search for the pig.

They sat down in a clearing and mashed maize and bread into a sticky paste in the enamel basin. In between trips to fetch water for the mix, they freely imbibed from the second bottle of poteen, and chased it down with bottles of frothy porter. When the mash was ready they laced it with a generous amount of spirit, but they made sure to keep an ample supply for themselves.

'Come on Curly Wee. Come an get it,' called Tom. 'Come on, Piggy Wiggy.'

'Be Jasus Dalt, he's going to be one mighty pissed pig when he gobbles up that lot,' Tom said, lifting the bottle of poteen to his lips again.

'Even if he gets half as "langers" as we are now, Tom, he's going to have a great time so he is. I wonder if pigs sing when they're pissed?'

They laid a trail of whiskey-mash away from the full basin of feed in the clearing, and hid behind a tree to wait and finish off the bottles. They sat with their backs to the tree-trunk and waited for the pig to emerge. But it wasn't the grunts and snuffles of the recalcitrant boar that awoke the echoes of the little island, but a rumbling noise from The Dalt and Tom Kennedy. The pair were still sitting with their backs against the tree, but deep in poteen-dreams, eyes closed, mouths open, and snoring as though their lives depended on it.

The six-o'clock deadline for the return of the cot passed and The Boy's patience ran out. He trudged home and outlined the story to Paddy, who was waiting patiently, ready to go fishing. Paddy listened until The Boy had finished, and then it mulled over for a long moment before speaking.

'You're sure they had what looked like two bottles of water with them as well?'

'Positive,' said The Boy, 'because Mr Rankin asked what they wanted water for when he had large bottles of stout ordered for them.'

'And what did they say to that?'

'The Dalt said that catching a pig was wicked thirsty work.'

'I see,' Paddy said scratching his head. 'You might as well go outside and play with your friends – we won't be going fishing this evening, I'm afraid.'

One afternoon, a week later, The Boy was doing his homework when he was surprised by a knock on the hall door, and even more surprised to see The Dalt standing on the doorstep.

'How's the second-best cot-man in the whole world? Is Moll inside?'

'Hello, Dalt. No, she isn't,' The Boy said, adding that she'd gone into town shopping with Maggie down the street, and wouldn't be back again till five.

'Here, so.' The Dalt handed him a large brown paper parcel. 'Give her that when she comes in – with my compliments.'

'What's in it?' The Boy asked. 'It's very heavy.'

'Well now, let me put it like this. I hope she's not gone shopping for pig meat. Tell her this stuff is flavoured from the inside out. And tell her as well that she should steep it well, because it's pickled with crude salt.'

Chapter 7

Harry's Haunting Tale

Paddy Whelan, The Dalt, Dave Wyse, Harry Duggan and The Boy were standing at the railings near Gashouse Bridge, watching the world go by or dally around them. Women pushed prams along the towpath or sat on the sun-scorched grass to play with their children. And as it was seven o'clock and a warm July evening, men walked along the quays with shirt sleeves rolled up and jackets slung over their shoulders. It was that lazy sort of evening most suited to convivial company and pleasant conversation.

'So you're telling me you don't go fishing at all now, Harry?' The Dalt remarked. He had just finished tackling-up the fishing rod and was waiting for a pocket of trout to start rising just ahead of the bridge. He had one eye trained on the river and an ear tuned to the story-swapping and remembered things their chat was made of.

'Naw, I don't bother with it any more. It's almost six years to the day since I last wet a line,' Harry drawled in a slow, matter-of-fact voice.

'You were a terrific angler altogether, so you were Harry,' Dave Wyse said. 'You could hold your own with the best of them on the Suir, or on any other river for that matter.' Dave turned to Paddy. 'He had a great cast, and could land a dryfly on the point of a needle. And if I'm not mistaken, he used to tie up his own troutflies too.' He turned again to Harry. 'Isn't that so, Harry?'

'You're not mistaken at all, Dave. I was accomplished with a fly rod but I don't know if I was as good as you say. I loved making the flies though. I must have tied up flies for half the anglers on the river.'

'That's true' said The Dalt, 'and he never took a single penny for one of them either.'

'I just did it for the sheer pleasure it gave me,' agreed Harry. 'Jasus but I used to love the bit of fishing after work in the evenings in particular. Ten minutes on the river and I was away in another world, with the trials and the tribulations of the day forgotten about. But I totally lost the heart for it. I don't feel a bit comfortable on the river anymore. Well, not on my own anyway. I'm just a bag of nerves now and that's the truth lads.'

'Did you fall in or did something else turn you off?' Paddy asked sympathetically.

'I'll put it like this Paddy. If I had a pound for every time I fell into that river I'd be a rich man today. No, it had nothing to do with that at all. It's easy to get over a wetting so it is.' Harry's voice trembled a little.

'Well, what in Christ's name happened to ya so, that turned you away from the sport you loved so much? A game that you were so shaggin' good at too,' Dave inquired, losing his patience with Harry.

'Jasus men, but me flesh crawls and shivers all over when I think about it,' Harry said, his drawl slowing even more.

'Are you going to tell us about what happened, before I lose my patience with you entirely?' The Dalt snapped.

'All right, all right. I'll tell you what happened. But let it be known that the only other person I ever told about this, over all the years, was the wife. She's dead and buried over three and a half years now, God be good to her.' Harry tipped his cap as a mark of respect. The Dalt took out a pack of Wild Woodbines and lit one, then offered the pack of cigarettes around. Dave politely refused one and Harry took out his pipe and began cutting a jot of tobacco with a penknife. He rubbed the tobacco into shreds in the palm of his hand before filling the pipe and lighting it.

''Twas a July evening not unlike this one,' Harry continued. 'It was very calm with plenty of heat in the air, ideal for a bit of dryfly fishing it was. I went home from a long hard day in the workshop after repairing the usual stuff that people bring in – kettles, pots and pans and the like. The same day I didn't finish until about quarter to seven and I went straight home. I didn't even stop off for a pint as I usually did. When I got home I asked herself to rustle me up something to eat because I was going down the river straightaway. I told her that I didn't want to waste too much time eating a big feed. So anyway, after the grub, I grabbed the rod, put the dog into the basket on the handlebars of the bike and off with me down the river, as happy as … Harry, I suppose you could say.'

'Was that the same little smooth-haired terrier with the split ear that you used to have?' asked Dave.

'It was. Skittles, I called her. The best little ratter that ever lived. She had no fear of anything at all in her. She'd go through hell and high water to get hold of a rat. Then when she caught one she'd give it a quick shake to kill it, then bring it back and drop it right at my feet to be praised for her efforts.'

Harry paused, and smiled to himself before continuing.

'Sometimes she'd drop a rat at our back door. Jasus, you'd want to hear the screams from the missus. You could hear the roars of her at the top of Irishtown. She'd leg it over to the workshop then and I'd have to leave everything and go back over to the house with her to get rid of the rat.'

'I remember that little dog well Harry,' Paddy said, thoughtfully. 'She was only a tiny little scrap of a thing, but fearless all right. She'd be sitting in the basket on the bike outside the workshop and if you as much as said boo to her, or got too near the bike, she'd bare the teeth and growl at you.'

'Yeah, that was her all right. She thought she owned that old bike. Anyway, there I was, full of the joys of summer, cycling away down to the river without a worry on my mind. When I got down to Killaloan I turned down the avenue and left the bike up against the fence at the side of the old graveyard. I'm telling you now lads, you couldn't get a better evening for fishing if you wrote away for it. There wasn't a puff of wind about, not a stir in the ivy on the ruins of the church, not a single leaf rustled in the trees. Do you know the ripples at the end of the first field, Dalt, where we cross over to the river after climbing over the big wrought iron gate?'

'Do I know them ripples? Do I know them?' The Dalt asked. 'The best spot on the river to get a few trout, especially when the water's low. There's a good bit of a hole there and it seems to hold a few trout there for some reason. A great spot!'

'You're on the ball, Dalt. You know exactly where I'm talking about. When I tackled up the rod, I sat down at the edge of the cowslip, lit up the pipe, and waited for the rise to start. Didn't have too long to wait either until a terrific spatter of trout started. A funny thing though, when I look back on it all now – the dog never bothered to go off hunting at all that evening, which was most unusual. She stayed at my heels all the time, and every now and then she'd let a whimper out of her. Of course, I didn't take a blind bit of notice at the time. I thought she had a thorn stuck in her paw or something. Anyway, before long I had three or four of the finest trout you ever laid eyes upon in the basket, none of them under a pound weight.'

'What were you getting them on?' The Dalt inquired, like any good angler would, trying to figure out what worked for another fisherman.

'I was catching them on a Red Spinner with a little gold tag on the tail, rather than the usual gold rib running up through the body. It was a pattern that I got from a Welsh fella who came over here to live when he retired. It's deadly in July so it is, when the spent duns are on the water in particular. You have to tie it up on a size sixteen hook though; anything bigger than that and it's a waste of time having it up at all. There's still a couple of them in the fly-box, Dalt. Call in some time whenever you're over my way and I'll give them to you because they're of no use to me now and that's for sure.'

'I'll do that Harry, thanks for the offer.'

'As I was saying, the light was beginning to fade a bit so I decided to put up a large Silver Horned Sedge so that I could see it better on the water in the dimming light. So, I wound in the line and sat down on the bank to tie on the Sedge. You can take the box of flies away with you too, Dalt, when you call.'

'Jasus Christ, Harry Duggan, will you get on with the shagging story and leave the flies for another time?' Dave Wyse piped up. 'I can't stand the suspense that you have me in any longer.'

'All right, all right. There I was, sitting beside the cowslip with one eye on a good lump of a trout that was rising a long ways out. He was feeding away nice and steady and I was trying to figure out the best way to cast over him. Then, whatever look I gave over my shoulder, I saw a man walking up along the bank of the river, and he was a good distance away at that stage. I recall thinking at the time that there was something very odd about him. The way that he moved maybe – an uncertain, unsteady, drifting kind of movement it was. It's hard to describe exactly what it was that made him look odd. But mark my words there was something very strange about him, even at that distance.

'The trout were rising away hot and heavy, so I shrugged it off and started to cast for the big trout that I was studying earlier. Now lads, this is where it got very eerie entirely. Can you visualise this? When I first saw this man he was about four or five hundred yards away from me. He was walking on the bend above the stream. I turned my back on him and started casting out to the big trout. Then, out of the blue and all of a sudden, he was standing only a few feet away from me, at my left shoulder. I needn't tell you boys, but I was flabbergasted. Flabbergasted, that's what I was. For the life of me, I couldn't figure out how he got so close to me, so fast. It was just impossible for any man to cover so much ground as quick as that.'

'Holy Jasus above in Heaven!' exclaimed Dave Wyse, beginning to walk away. 'I don't like the way this yarn is shaping up at all at all. I don't want to hear any more about this kind of stuff, I'm off.'

'Hold it! Stay right where you are,' Harry said sternly. 'Don't move another inch, Dave Wyse, until you hear precisely what I have to say. And let's get one thing straight here and now. This is not a yarn. It's a fact. It actually happened. So you'll stay here and listen to the truth for a change – it's high time you heard some of it.'

'Don't lose your hair, Harry. There's no need to get upset. I'll stay put,' Dave said, a bit shocked at the intensity of Harry's censure.

'I'm sorry I snapped at you, Dave, but I still get upset over it, so please forgive me.'

'No apology necessary, Harry. Go ahead, auld stock.'

'"A very good evening to you sir", I said to him. But he didn't reply. Not one word of any sort did I get from him. So I says, "It's a great day entirely, sir", but he still said nothing. Well men, let me tell you this: all of a sudden the air around me turned stone cold. The hair on the back of my neck and arms stood up tingling. I felt icy, yet the sweat was running down my back like a stream. Immediately after I spoke to him he slipped behind me and then, for a second or two, I felt the faintest breeze and there was a mildewed, acidy kind of smell in the air. It was like the smell you get from old damp books. But it didn't linger. It was there and then it was gone again in the blink of an eye. I turned around as fast as I could to see which direction he was heading in, but there was no sight, sound nor trace of him anywhere. He just disappeared – vanished into thin air.'

'Did he fall into the river or what?' The Dalt asked.

'If he fell into the water, I'd have heard a splash, but there was none. There was no disturbance of any kind, Dalt. But what happened next really put the tin hat on it and convinced me I was dealing with someone, or something, that was not of this world at all.'

'Oh suffering Jasus, Harry.' The Dalt looked and sounded uneasy. 'You're putting the heart cross-ways in me, but go on.'

'Whatever glance I gave over my shoulder, Skittles, my brave and fearless terrier was running across the field as fast as her little legs could carry her, and the hair was standing straight up on her back like the spines on a hedgehog. I never saw her running so fast before, or after for that matter either. Well, that was enough for me. There and then, I dropped the rod on the spot where I was standing and legged it as fast as I possibly could back across the field to the bike. I didn't look left or right because there was only one thing on my mind then and that was to get out of there. I can tell you one thing now lads, and I don't mind admitting it. But I was glad I had bicycle clips on my trousers on the way home, because the shit was well and truly frightened out of me, so it was. When I got back to the house, the dog was curled up into a ball on the doorstep, shivering and shaking, a nervous wreck. When I got into the house herself took one look at me.

'"What in Christ's name happened to you, Harry Duggan", she said. "You look like you're just after seeing a ghost".'

Chapter 8

The Sluice-Hole Caper

'Evening all.' The Dalt stood framed in the doorway, tipping his cap. It was his trademark salutation on arrival at Whelan's Forge for the nightly card-game. Paddy and Moll were already there, warming themselves at the fire. Cheerful Stephen Hannigan, Mick Whelan and a gentleman known as The Whippet arrived in soon afterwards. They were there to chat and play cards. It was the way of things at night in Whelan's Forge. The forge was their meeting-place after a hard day's work. The sound of the anvil was replaced by the chatter of card-players into the small hours, and the clatter of winning hands coming down, knuckles-first, on the tabletop. But there was more than cards on the agenda this night.

Stephen winked at The Dalt, carefully slipped a small parcel from under his coat, and concealed it behind the cooling cask. The cards were shuffled and the game began in earnest, accompanied by the mandatory card-game squabbles, precipitated by accusations of 'bad play' or crooked dealing. The hours ticked away. Several times during the night, Mick went over to the window and looked out over the forge pool towards the sluice-hole. During the day the sluice-hole was practically dry, and only a trickle of water went through it. Children safely played there at low water, jumping from stone to stone in games of 'don't get your feet wet', while the older ones hunted for crayfish or stabbed flatfish with a dinner fork lashed to a broom handle. At night the hole filled up when two mills on the river above it opened their sluice gates and released water back into the river system again. The hole was long and narrow and about six or seven feet deep at high water. Salmon and trout moved in there as it filled up, a respite from the strong run on the river.

It was past midnight when Mick Whelan threw in the cards.

'I'm off,' he said, 'it's getting late.' That was a signal for the others. Ten minutes before that he had strolled over to the window and noticed that the water in the sluice hole had reached its peak. He knew then it was time to make a move.

'I'll go with ya,' said The Dalt.

'I'm away as well,' said Stephen. 'Are you coming with us, Whippet?'

'Yeah, I'm with you.'

'Where are you lot off to so early?' Paddy asked. 'It's usually two or more in the morning before you head off to your beds.'

'We'll drop in again tomorrow night, Paddy.' The Dalt said, giving nothing away. Stephen strolled over to the cooling barrel and slipped the parcel under his coat. Outside, away from the smouldering embers of the forge, there was a distinct September chill in the night air. They sniffed the air like badgers coming out of a den, wary of unwanted company.

'Jasus lads,' said Stephen, 'I'm not so sure about this caper now. It's after getting a hell of a lot brighter since I looked out of the forge window last. There's too much moonlight shining and those clouds up there are a bit flimsy.'

'We'll need that light,' Mick said. 'It's now or never, lads. There've been six or seven salmon in and out of that hole over there for the last three days. I have clients standing in line with money in their pockets to take them off our hands. I'm sure we could all do with the extra few shillings.'

'None of us are here for the fun of it alone, Mick,' Stephen said. 'But how do we know the fish are not gone upriver to the spawning reds?'

'That's a stupid question, especially coming from a man born, bred and reared beside the river,' Mick snapped. 'Those salmon are going nowhere till they get plenty of rain. There's not enough water in the main river to let them through the gap in the weir.'

'He's spot on Stephen,' said The Dalt. 'Now: are we or ain't we going to do it, because I'm not standing around here till dawn waiting for a decision. Anyway, I need beer money. I'm flat broke so I am.'

'Let's get on with it then,' Mick said decisively. 'I'll go down and push Paddy's cot up and moor it in behind the bushes at the island wall. Whippet, you know what to do, so away with you now and get on with it. Dalt, you go with Stephen and get across that bridge but don't be seen. Go down to the end of Mill Lane, circle around the side of the Mill and get in over the red gate. Cross over to the pool, and be sure to stay well out of sight behind the storage huts. Hide behind the wheelhouse shed until you see my signal. Two long flashes. When you see that it's your cue to lay the net along the shore down to the end of the sluice hole. Tie the ropes to the trunk of the sycamore and then sit into the cot with me.'

Mick was like a commando captain leading his men on a nocturnal raid deep into enemy territory. He turned to Stephen.

'Now Stephen, pay heed to this. There's one minor adjustment in the plan that applies to you in particular. Whatever happens, don't even attempt to effect your end of the job until you see one long flash from the lamp. One long flash. If I give two short flashes that's your signal to abandon everything there and then and get straight down to the cot. But if all goes well – which it will, of course – and you have your final deed done, get down to the net, untie it from the tree and hold on tight.'

'I thought we were going to bag-up the catch at the Sluices and then scamper back out the way we came in?' Stephen was taken aback that the plan had been changed without consultation. 'And weren't we supposed to leave the cot there as a decoy, as if it was stolen?'

'Trust me Stephen and just do as I ask, will you?' Mick pleaded.

'I hope that shagging net is where it's supposed to be,' The Dalt added. He too was concerned with the alteration to the plans.

'It's in the bunker behind the tool shed, Dalt, exactly where I said it would be. I saw Billy Burke putting it in there himself at eight o'clock this very evening when he was greasing the cogs on the upper sluices. But just to make sure he did exactly as I told him, I sat on the wall across from the weir and watched him. Are you happy now?' There was an irate, impatient edge in Mick's voice.

'Are you sure he'll keep his mouth shut about it?' Stephen asked. 'He wouldn't be my first choice of a partner in crime, and that's for sure. He has a wicked big trap on him, especially when he has a few jars inside.'

'Well, for one thing Stephen, he's in on a cut from the profits. And for another thing, he was the only man I knew working in the mill who wouldn't draw attention to himself going down to the sluices carrying a canvas bag over his shoulder. So rest at ease lads. Mr Burke and myself have an agreement that should prove to be of great advantage to each of us before the dawn breaks.'

Unknown to them all, Mick had given Billy Burke strange instructions that previous afternoon, telling him to go into the Mill

Bar and boast openly about his collusion in the raid.

'And don't forget to give Hartigan the red herring,' Mick said to Burke, with a promise of a bonus payment for spinning the barman a bogus version of the plan – information that would lay down a false scent. What Burke didn't know was that Mick had a grand plan up his sleeve, which exploited a long-standing friendship between Hartigan, the barman, and O'Shea, the local water bailiff. Mick had charmed Hartigan's girlfriend away from him some years before, and he was hoping that Hartigan would grasp the opportunity to try and even up the score. He was confident that Hartigan would inform on him; in fact, he was very much depending on it.

When Mick pulled the cot in at the rendezvous, his arms ached. The flow was particularly strong along The Orchard run and fierce over the sunken weir at the forge. The Dalt and Stephen arrived at the sluice gates as Mick pulled in further down. They had climbed over the red gate beside the mill and lay low on the grass. Silent but nervous, they waited patiently for Mick's signal. Forty-five nerve-shattering minutes elapsed before they saw the signal, one, and then, two flashes.

'It's go,' The Dalt whispered.

'I thought he'd never signal,' Stephen said, shaking from head to toe. They rolled out the net and The Dalt pulled it over the grass and down along the shore to the moored cot. Mick was waiting and as The Dalt tied one set of ropes to the sycamore tree, Mick folded the bulk of the net over the gunnels, ready to slip it into action. When they had the net ready, both of them stepped into the cot and waited.

Mick stood in the stern with the pole and The Dalt sat on the bow-seat holding onto the slack net ropes. Although the air was cold, Stephen perspired as he waited for Mick's signal. He thought that he heard a noise in the distance and feared it was the bailiff's car. But he managed to ignore it and finish what he was doing. Mick fixed his gaze on the second-floor windows of a house in Weir View Terrace, and waited for the signal that could prove to be the most decisive of the entire operation.

The Whippet, from his vantage point on the top floor of No 9 Weir View Terrace, had a clear view across two bridges where they converged on the laneway beside the mill. He watched O'Shea, the bailiff, park his car a safe distance from the laneway and then move into position to ambush the poachers as they made their exit through the lane. Unaware that The Whippet was observing every move that he made, the bailiff rubbed his hands together with delight. He could almost taste success. Those reprobates had eluded him for years and here they were at last within his grasp. O'Shea chuckled to himself. He couldn't fail this time, for he'd carefully followed the trail of information received, and had two policemen lying-in-wait for the poachers beside the red gate.

The Whippet saw the policemen walking across the bridge. He ran down the stairs two at a time, jumped on his bicycle and took off at speed towards the mill. He spent a short time there and then did a U-turn back over the bridge. He pulled up on the centre arch of the next bridge where Mick would clearly see his signal. He looked around to make sure that the coast was clear and then he sent three short flashes, followed by one long flash.

'Good on you, Whippet, me auld pal, me auld stock,' Mick muttered, then turned with a note of decisiveness in his voice. 'Get ready, Dalt. The real fun is about to start.'

'Ready, but my teeth are chattering like castanets,' The Dalt croaked. Mick pointed the lamp at the sluice hole and sent the code to Stephen, then immediately started poling for the middle of the river. The Dalt held onto the snap ropes on the net as securely as he could and braced himself against the pull of the water. The net unfurled into the river, and his knuckles turned white from the strain as they towed it out.

Stephen's hands shook as he lit the fuse on the first stick of dynamite and tossed the charge into the pool at the head of the sluice. Ten seconds later he sparked a charge with a shorter fuse, and threw that in as well. Then he lay face down on the grass. The explosives went off with a loud thump rather than an earth-shattering bang. It was heard back at the forge.

'God Almighty, what was that — a clap of thunder?' Paddy Whelan asked, fearfully.

'It didn't sound like thunder to me, Paddy,' said Moll.

'Christ, Moll,' Paddy was white in the face. 'I know now what Stephen had in that little bundle of his, and why he was so secretive about his little parcel. The buggers are just after blasting the sluice hole; they've blown it up.'

'Jesus, Mary and holy Saint Joseph,' Moll screamed, 'are they stark raving mad or what? If they get caught they'll go to jail, the whole bloody lot of them.' Paddy ran out the doorway and down the steps onto the riverbank. He had a gut feeling that the boys would make their way back to the arch under the gable of the house.

After the explosion, Stephen felt dizzy and disorientated. Although he had covered his ears before the bang, he couldn't hear very well, and his head was reeling from the blast. But he managed to run down and untie the net from the tree trunk and hold the ropes firmly against the pull of the cot and the current. Stunned salmon and trout began to surface in the sluice-hole and they drifted down into the main channel of the river. Mick steered the cot into position and circled around the fish with the net.

'Christ Almighty, Mick,' gasped The Dalt. 'Will you look at the amount of salmon on top of the water? Six or seven me arse! There must be twenty or more.'

'So what if I can't count,' Mick said, poling hard for the sycamore tree. When they reached the bank, The Dalt jumped out and helped Stephen haul the net high and dry. They had to work fast, for the fish were beginning to recover from the shock waves and were already thrashing about wildly in the net.

'Cull six cock fish but leave the hens alone. Be fast now.'

'But, Mick, why only six? There's buckets of them?' said Stephen.

'I have a definite market for six fish, so leave the rest to multiply and increase. Nature's law Stephen: waste not want not.'

O'Shea, the bailiff, and his assistants continued their surveillance on the red gate. When they heard the bang, they calculated that it would take the poachers about thirty-five minutes to gather up the fish and reach the gate.

'I don't want any mistakes now,' O'Shea told the policemen. 'I've been waiting for years to catch these bastards. Stay where you are until they climb out over that gate, then pounce on them. Use your truncheons if you have to. They'll have no other escape route once they're in the lane – it's a dead end.'

As the bailiff spoke, the last of six large salmon had been loaded on board the cot and the poachers had pushed off from the bank.

'What? What's that you said, Mick?' Stephen roared. 'I can't hear a shagging thing you're saying. There's a ceilí band playing away at full-tilt inside my head. I think it might be the Kilfenora.' He laughed out loud, high as a kite on the adrenaline surging through him.

'Will you keep quiet for Christ's sake, Stephen, or you'll get us all jailed.'

'Sorry, Mick.'

The Dalt paddled with all his might and Mick poled furiously down and across the river towards the forge. Stephen put three big rocks into a sack, tied the neck securely and threw it overboard. They would retrieve the net when the heat died down. They crossed over the final bit of turbulence into the calmer waters of the Mill Stream and Mick turned the nose of the cot under the arch at the gable end of the forge.

'Jesus, I hope there's none of them inside bursting for a piss, or we'll be scalded to death.' Mick laughed loudly, more in satisfaction at pulling-off the caper than at his own crude joke.

The minutes ticked by and it eventually dawned on O'Shea, the bailiff, that the poachers were not about to make their escape by the anticipated route.

'They're after pulling the wool over our eyes,' he snapped at the lawmen. 'Back to the car quick. There's only one place these bastards will head for. I should've guessed.'

Paddy Whelan and The Whippet were waiting when the cot pulled in under the arch.

'Did The Whippet fill you in, Paddy?' Mick inquired.

'There was no need, you hare-brained bloody lunatic. I put two and two together myself when I heard the thud.' Paddy growled, pointing his finger menacingly. 'If you damaged that cot, I'll swing for you, brother or no brother.'

'Not even a plank blown off her, brother,' Mick said, slipping the rope through a mooring ring. 'Here Paddy, put that fish into the sack will you, and don't start lecturing me about the difference between right and wrong. Would it be too much to ask you to wash any remaining evidence out of your own cot – blood and scales and the like, please – while we scamper away with the real proof?'

'That's one mighty lump of a salmon, Mick, there's twenty pounds in him at least,' Paddy said, lowering it into the sack.

'A far better one altogether slipped over the rim of the net before The Dalt could raise the top rope high enough to trap him. There was at least thirty pounds in him.' Mick stretched his arms out, the way fishermen do.

'He was the finest salmon I've ever seen in all my days on the Suir, or any other river for that matter,' The Dalt agreed.

O'Shea and the policemen arrived breathlessly back at the car and discovered that the front tyres were as flat as pancakes. O'Shea kicked the car, hard.

'They think they're bloody smart, do they now?' he said, expletives and spittle showering the two policemen.

'Get over to the barracks straightaway and get a warrant to search Whelan's Forge. No, get a warrant to search the forge and the whole fucking house as well.'

'I don't think so, sir,' said one of the policemen.

'Are you disobeying my orders?'

'No, sir.'

'Well, do it now, then.'

'Not much point, sir.'

'Are you sure you and your colleague over there are actually assigned to this operation?'

'We are sir.'

'Then get on with it, man!'

'Sorry, sir. But as I said, there's not much point really, sir.'

'What do you mean, not much point?'

'Our Superior Officer, sir.'

'Your Superior Officer what, my good man?'

'He's not available at this hour of the morning, sir. Tucked up nice and comfy in his warm bed, sir, I reckon.'

'Very well then. We'll just have to go and get him out of his cosy little bed then, won't we, officer?'.

'Not much chance of that, sir.'

'And why not?' O'Shea bellowed.

'He lives a long way out of town, sir. Near Fethard.'

'Well, drive out there and get him then!'

'Can't, sir.'

'What the flaming hell do you mean, can't?'

'Only one car in the barracks, sir, and he's got it.'

'Well, take mine then, you stupid idiot.'

'Can't, sir. Flat tyres, sir.'

'Bollocks.'

The following Saturday night The Dalt, Stephen, Mick and The Whippet met in the Mill Bar to divide up the profits from the raid on the sluice hole.

'So the three flashes from the bridge meant that they were waiting up the lane for us, is that right, Mick?'

'Correct, Stephen. And the final signal from The Whippet, before I flashed you at the sluice hole, told me that he had let the air out of the tyres. It's like this men, plain and simple. I was told – sorry, I should say that I was reliably informed – that O'Shea was sniffing around during the week. Now, whether he got wind of the job or not, I'm not certain – but I wanted to know precisely where O'Shea would be when the job was going down.' Mick explained.

'As it turned out, he was well and truly out of the way where I put him, especially with no transport available to him.'

'Why didn't you fill myself and Stephen in on the full plan?' The Dalt asked.

'Yourself and Stephen were a bag of nerves all week,' Mick explained. 'If you knew that O'Shea was going to be in such close proximity to us, beside us almost, you'd probably have wanted to back out of the whole thing.'

'You're spot on there, Mick,' Stephen cut in. 'Sure, you would-n't have seen me for dust.'

'If it went wrong for any reason,' Mick continued, 'I figured we could keep sailing on down the river until it was safe to come ashore. O'Shea had no car, thanks to you Whippet, and I knew that the law had none either. And there was no way he could have got to us fast enough without a car.'

'Jesus Mick, but you're as cute as a room full of scholars,' The Dalt said, with a grin as wide as an arch on Gashouse Bridge.'

'Barman,' Mick shouted at the top of his voice so that every-one in the bar heard him. 'Three hot toddies, and please, be so kind as to take for the price of one for our esteemed friend, the bailiff, Mr O'Shea. I have been reliably informed that he picked up a nasty chill the other night for some reason.' Several customers who knew about the raid burst out laughing.

'He'll get you yet, and I'll get you back too, Whelan. Mark my words. Just you mark my words,' the barman said, venomously.

'Yes indeed, that possibility always exists. Miracles happen every day of the week,' said Mick. 'But there's one thing sure and certain, Mr Hartigan.'

'And what would that be, Whelan?'

'You won't ever get your girlfriend back. Cheers lads.'

Chapter 9

Michael Dwyer and the River

Warm riverwater sang with benzodiazepine in Michael Dwyer's brain. Bright lights flashed and colours sped before his eyes. The voices in his head were screaming whispers now.

Let go! Abandon all your pain and suffering.

Escape the emptiness.

Follow the lights and you'll find peace!

'I must escape. I must let go.'

The voices were a screaming chorus of approval.

Now! Let go now. Do it now! Drain the septic pool of bitter memories!

'Thou shalt not covet thy neighbour's wife. They fucked me up and signed my life away and threw away the key.'

Michael, the words are written, the ink is dry.

They pronounce you insane, leave you with nothing.

'Damn them! Damn them both! My Judas brother. My Jezebel wife. Our Father who art in heaven forgive us our trespasses.' And the waters of the living river closed around him.

Yes, yes! Do it now, Michael! Escape the emptiness! Do it now!

And warm riverwater sang with benzodiazepine in Michael Dwyer's brain.

The Boy and his friends were playing skittles on the street when two policemen came round the corner and stopped outside Paddy Whelan's house.

'There's no one inside,' he said before they could knock on the door. He thought they'd come about the eels he'd put through Dan Murphy's door in revenge for taking his football.

'We want to speak to Paddy,' the sergeant said authoritatively.

'What about?' The Boy asked.

'Well now, that's really none of your business,' the sergeant said. Then his face broke into a smile. 'But I want to see him about doing a little job for me.'

'Now that I think of it, my Aunt Moll could have gone back inside without me seeing her.' The Boy amended his story and ran inside to tell Moll that the Guards were waiting at the front door.

'Tell them to come inside,' she said. 'I have a fair idea what they want.'

'Welcome Tom, and who's this new Guard with you – is he here to interrogate me?' Moll asked.

'Moll, this is Noel Brosnan, all the way from Cork. Noel, this is Mollie Whelan, better known as Moll. She makes the best apple tarts in Ireland so she does, and in her day she cooked for the aristocracy in England.'

'You're more than welcome, Noel,' Moll said. 'We won't hold it against you that you're from Cork. Sit down there now the pair of ye and have some tea and scones. Put on the kettle, son.'

'Did you hear the bad news, Moll?' The sergeant took off his black peak cap and tucked it under his arm.

'No Tom, but I know why you're here. The river has claimed some other poor soul, hasn't it?'

'That's the broad and the long of it Moll,' the new Guard said.

'Michael Dwyer, a patient out of the mental hospital. The poor chap threw himself off the Old Bridge, God help him. A few people that were walking at the time saw it happening. The strange thing though is this, they said he didn't surface again, not even once. He went down and stayed down.'

'That's not uncommon Noel,' Moll said. 'If his mind was set on it, he'd make no attempt at all to save himself. He'd just let himself go, drift away with the river.'

'I never heard that before, Moll,' said Tom. 'I thought he'd come to the surface at some stage. Anyway, we shouldn't be talking like this in front of the young lad there.'

'Don't worry Tom, he knows about these things. He has the river in his blood, just like his Uncle Paddy has. It's not the first nor the last time he'll hear about it.'

The sergeant took a deep breath and shook his head.

'It's the total unnecessary waste of life that gets to me,' he said. 'But then, I suppose, no one really understands the dark mind of a suicide, do they Moll? I wonder what drove poor Michael Dwyer to it? Maybe he suffered pain and turmoil beyond our comprehension and unfortunately any cry for help went unheard or unheeded. But I suppose we'll never know.'

The Boy, who'd been standing quietly next to the table, suddenly piped up.

'Uncle Paddy told me that hundreds of years ago in Ireland the high priests sacrificed people to the river gods because they had to satisfy their hunger for human spirits. And if they didn't make regular sacrifices the gods would get very angry and drown loads of people from the tribe.'

'Well now,' said the sergeant, 'there could be some truth in it, because that river of ours claims several lives every year. I often wonder though, does the river claim them or do the river gods show mercy and receive them.' The last of what he said was accompanied by a noise from outside.

'That's Paddy coming for a bite to eat now, Tom,' Moll said. 'That old bread van he drives makes an awful racket entirely. It's high time they bought a new one for him.' Paddy looked at the guards and threw his eyes heavenwards.

'Who's in the river?' he asked, leaning against the frame of the door.

'It's a patient from the mental hospital, Paddy,' sergeant Tom said. 'Young enough he was too. Not much with forty years of age. I'm sure you saw him often enough around the town. He wasn't a violent man by any means. In fact, he was the complete opposite and they allowed him out two or three times a week to do a bit of shopping and stuff like that.'

'Did he wear a tweed cap and brown gabardine coat all the time?' Paddy asked.

'He did indeed, Paddy. The matron told us that he suffered from bouts of depression and anxiety. They had him on drugs all the time to try and control it. It seems his condition was sparked off in the first instance by some family feud over land. Anyway, whatever it was, he took to the drink over it and in the heel of the hunt his wife signed him into the mental hospital. He'd been in there for the last fifteen years.' The sergeant paused for a shudder. 'Can you imagine that – fifteen years?'

'Nothing new in that Tom,' Moll said. 'There's several cases just like that in every mental hospital in the country. No one should have that right, that kind of clout, to sign another human being into a mental institution for their own self-centred needs. It's just not right, Tom. I know of one particular case like that, not too far from where I was reared either. A big farmer declared his own daughter insane because she wanted to marry a young lad that her family thought was below their status in life. That poor girl spent seven years in a mental hospital and she only got out when both her parents had passed away. She never got married though, and she was never really happy again either. She tried to join an order of nuns but they wouldn't accept her because she had a history of mental illness. Christianity my arse, Tom – excuse the language.'

'That's sad, Moll, very sad indeed,' the new Garda said.

'Tom, whereabouts did this poor chap throw himself in?' Paddy inquired.

'At the Old Bridge. They're dragging along the strand, down as far as the bridge as we speak.'

'I don't think his body will hold up along there, Tom. The currents are very strong along that stretch.'

'Well, that's why we called on you. No one knows that part of the river better than yourself. Will you come down after work and show us where to look?'

'Christ Almighty, Tom, but I loathe this kind of thing. I've taken too many bodies out of the river and it gets harder each time. But if you think I can help you, then so be it. I'll offer it up for me sins.'

'Thanks,' the sergeant said, shaking Paddy's hand.

'Don't mention it, Tom. For now, I suggest that you move the whole operation downriver and start dragging at the top of the Mill Pond. Start below the Gashouse Bridge, at the dog track. Concentrate all you're efforts on the Tipperary shore for the time being and I'll try to get away from work as early as I can to join you.'

'Thanks again, Paddy,' said Tom.

'No thanks needed Tom, and if you want the cot in the mean-time, Huck here can go down to the mooring and get it ready for you. But he's not to go out searching under any circumstances.'

'Aw, Uncle Paddy, why not?' The Boy protested.

'I said no, and that's final. It's not a pleasant experience to see a body dragged from the river. Anyway, you'll be needed on the shore.'

The Boy stood on the bank and watched the boatmen cast their ropes into the water. The ropes were weighted down with strips of lead and studded with large, three-pronged fishing-hooks. They cast the ropes in and retrieved them slowly, systematically dragging the Mill Pond in the hope of snagging the body. One of the cots searched the margins of the riverbank, the men probing with long thin poles through the roots of trees and under the matted beds of river weeds. Their job was painstaking and arduous.

When Paddy arrived on the bank, he called the boatmen ashore to discuss what they should do next. The Boy doled out tea and sandwiches for the crews before they returned to the river. Very few of them had much appetite for food. They ate sparingly and pushed off to search again. When the shadows of the big chestnuts began to creep across the river, the crews were called in for the day. They tied their boats up and stood on the riverbank, their conversation hushed and reverent, and underscored by disappointment.

'There's one sure thing,' The Whippet said, pointing up the river. 'He's not at the top of that pond. Four times we're after dragging it, left, right and centre. He's not there and that's all about it. We should concentrate lower down in the morning.'

'What d'you think of that suggestion, Paddy?' asked the sergeant.

'It's as good a suggestion as any. If we don't find his body there, we can be fairly certain that he's gone over the weir. If that's the case it's going to be one hell of a job trying to figure out where the poor bastard is wedged up.'

The first stars reflected in the water as they made their way home. Bats and moths flew around, and trout were rising freely to black midges and Swirling Evening Duns. At any other time, The Boy's heart would have quickened with desire to be out on the river, tempting the trout. But, as much as any of the men, he too was cloaked in the dark shadow cast by the suicide of poor Michael Dwyer.

'Uncle Paddy?'

'Yes, Huck.'

'I've never seen so many cots tied up together in the one spot before.'

'Well, that's the nature of our river folk, Huck. They always pull together at times like these. Everyone who was out dragging that river today, myself included, hates the job. But we won't shy away from it, either. It upsets us all to the core but it must be done.' He paused for a moment, then pointed out towards the river. 'I love that river, Huck, but this very minute, I'm maddened by it. Angry to the point that I want to scream at it. Why won't the bitch give up the body without a battle, just this once?'

'Maybe the river gods are hungry again, Uncle Paddy?'

The search for Michael Dwyer got under way again next day at the crack of dawn. Teams dragged every square foot of the river-bottom on the top and lower sections of the Mill Pond, but the Suir would not relent. The search intensified and during the days that followed, extra boats and fresh crews joined in. Day after long weary day, volunteers walked the riverbank looking for a sign, however insignificant, that might lead to the discovery of the body. On the eighth day, as late evening shadows stretched across the river, the dark silhouette of failure lay ever more heavily on the shoulders of the searchers, and haunted their pale, drawn faces. Sergeant Tom called the crews together to discuss what they should do next. There was a worried, thoughtful quiet, then a murmuring that seemed to knit itself into one voice. They knew what they must do. If the body wasn't recovered next day – the ninth day – they'd float the lights.

Chapter 10

Floating the Lights

A sheaf of river reeds tumbled across the scrubbed oak table in Mary Guiry's kitchen. The table had been her grandmother's, and her great-grandmother's before that. They'd had the gift too. Mary remembered Grandma Guiry sitting at the table, sorting the reeds into bundles. She always sat in the same corner, always said the same prayer. A faint acerbic smell of carbolic soap rising from the aged wood under her fingertips brought her back to the task in hand.

She remembered the last one that she had made. It was for that little boy, the son of a fisherman. He was on the Quay, worm-fishing for trout. It was May. There was a flood. He lost his footing and tumbled in. His friends ran to get help but the fierce river swept him away. It was the ninth day when his parents called. She'd never be able to put that day out of her mind. The pain burned like phosphorous in their eyes. Their faces said it all. They were frantic to find him and give him a Christian burial. And now here she was again, feeling the distress and depression of another body in the river.

'This is neither a gift nor a blessing – it's a curse,' she said aloud and fumbled with the pile of reeds on the table. But as she twisted the reeds into the shape of a cross, she felt the blessing of her gift and the rhythm of her fingers harmonised with a prayer on her lips.

'Christ, who walked on the waters of Galilee, pray for me. Saint Peter the fisherman, find Michael Dwyer who's lost in the river below this town. Bless this wreath, in the name of the Father, the Son and the Holy Ghost. Amen.'

'Well now, Mary Guiry, but aren't you the strange kettle of fish. Do you mean to tell me that after all these years you're still afraid to go out there in that cot?' Paddy Whelan was standing with Mary on the riverbank. 'Are you sure it's not me that you're afraid of? Maybe it's the temptation of the two of us out there together, alone in a little boat that bothers you?'

'Go way out of that, Paddy Whelan,' Mary giggled. 'Though if you weren't spoken for, who knows? But seriously now, Paddy, I am afraid of the water. If the truth be known, I'm actually scared stiff of it. Maybe when God burdened me with this gift, he also gave me the fear of water. I wonder was that his own peculiar way of protecting me from it? But I've seen too many corpses dragged out over the years and when some poor soul comes to the door these days asking for help, I have to force meself to give it.'

'Mary, I understand,' Paddy said. 'I didn't mean to be flippant. I'm sorry, it was very insensitive of me. But tell me this, what do we do now? Do we follow the same procedure we followed when we found that little lad?'

'To be honest, Paddy, I don't really know. I have a feeling that his body was around here, and for quite some time too. But I think it's moved on again. No use in floating the lights here. Let's try further down.'

They walked at funeral-pace along the bank. She held a rosary beads in one hand and a wreath of river reeds in the other, and stopped often to listen to the murmurings of the Suir. Now and then, she sat down on the riverbank, closed her eyes and remained motionless for five or ten minutes at a time. The men in cots knew their place in the ritual and followed along at a distance behind her. When she was ready to pin down an area where the body was likely to be, the boats would move in and mark it. The sergeant, the Three Wise Men and The Boy followed behind.

'Keep on stuffing the grub into the boatmen Huck, it's hungry bloody work this,' Paddy said. 'And one other thing,' he added, as he pulled away from shore. 'If we happen to find that poor man, I don't want to see you within a long bawl of the leading boat. If I do I'll come ashore myself and kick the arse off you.'

'What he advised is definitely for your own good, lad,' Dave Wyse said. 'After this length of time in the water, it won't be a pretty sight.'

'He's dead right there, so he is,' Simon Wyse added. 'It wouldn't do you any good at all.'

'Yeah,' James Wyse chimed, 'what with the rats an' the currents after draggin' him over rocks, he could be in an awful state altogether so he could. He won't even be recognisable. I remember the first time I saw a body taken outa that river there. I wasn't much older than you are now, young fella. It was a young woman, so it was. The poor bitch was in there for two weeks and two days. God Almighty, but I got the gawks straight away, so I did. I puked me guts up and then started shaking like a leaf in the wind. And that's the way I was for a long time after – gawking and shaking.'

'For Christ's sake, lads, leave that poor young fella alone,' the sergeant cut in angrily. 'You'll have the life frightened out of him.'

'There's no need to lose your rag, Tim. We're only trying to protect the lad's innocence,' Simon pointed out.

'We're all a bit edgy after the last few days. I'm sorry that I spoke to you like that,' Tim said, apologetically.

Mary Guiry slowly paced up and down a section of the riverbank. She was nervous and hesitant, as though awaiting some revelation. Suddenly, her whole body shuddered and the rosary beads fell from her fingers. She walked over to the hedge behind her, broke off a hawthorn twig and pushed it into the soil as a marker where the rosary beads had fallen. Dazed and disorientated, she moved off towards a small dyke that drained the marsh fields into the river, but fell to her knees before she reached it. The Sergeant watched her and could only think of a wounded bird. He made a movement to help her but Dave put a restraining hand on his arm.

'No, Tim, leave it be. There's nothing wrong with her. She's getting close – very close.'

'But she needs help,' Tim said. 'She looks terrible.'

'I know what I'm talking about, Tim. I've seen her doing this kind of thing before. Just leave her be. If they need us down there they'll call us.'

Mary got to her feet and snapped another stem from a bush to mark the ground again, then signalled to Paddy to come ashore.

When they had walked between the two markers several times, she rummaged in her pockets to find and light the blessed candles. She put them in a glass holder, pushed them into the centre of the wreath, then knelt down and prayed. She handed the wreath to Paddy and told him where to begin floating the lights. Paddy waved to the crewmen in the leading cot and they came ashore.

'I'm going to start floating the reeds at the fence over there,' he said. 'And I have to do it in accordance with Mary's instructions. That means I have to float the wreath three times, three lights, to symbolise the Divine Trinity – Father, Son and Holy Ghost. I'm going to send them out from three different points contained by the boundaries she's laid down. Now – ' he paused dramatically –

'keep your eyes on Mary at all times, and if she signals for you to pole over a particular spot, do it straight away. Hold your position there and make sure that you don't drift away from it. We may not get a second crack at this.'

Paddy set the wreath afloat from the centre of the river and it drifted on past the lower marker uninterrupted. With the following drift the wreath veered over to the opposite shore, and staggered briefly on the surface before moving off again. Mary called the men and asked them to hold steady in that area. Released for the third time, the wreath gyrated slowly and the flames flickered and died. Paddy spoke with Mary for several minutes, then made his way up the bank to join the others.

'She reckons he'll be found within a thirty feet radius of the markers,' he told the sergeant. 'It's pretty deep water along there, though – ten to fifteen feet in places. Another two or three boats wouldn't go astray to help cover that amount of water before dark.'

'Is she positive that the body is there, Paddy?'

'As sure as she can be, Tim. She's drained from the effort that she's put into it. The poor girl is very upset after it all, she's all-in. Exhausted. Anyway,' he turned to the rest of the men. 'I've done my bit, so I'm going home now. I've no stomach for dragging that body from the river.'

'We'll bring Mary up to the pub and throw hot port and brandy into her until she gets her strength back,' said Simon Wyse.

'Leave her in our capable hands,' his brother,' Dave said.

'We'll look after her the same way we look after ourselves,' added James, the third brother.

'That's what worries me,' the sergeant commented, a thin smile breaking over his gaunt face.

Chapter 11

Paddy Rises to the Bait

'Paddy's having an attack of the nerves, Simon,' Moll said. 'He dragged that auld river once too often for his own good.'

It was her stock, unabashed reply when asked why he wasn't out fishing. Simon Wyse nodded understandingly and walked slowly down the street. He met The Dalt coming from the opposite direction and told him the news about Paddy Whelan.

'Dragging the river precipitated a descent into dark melancholy, Dalt.'

'He's having an attack of the nerves,' The Dalt answered, translating on the hoof.

But Moll knew deep down that the affair of Michael Dwyer was merely the catalyst, not the cause. Problems at work and the onset of coronary disease had been weighing heavily upon him, and the river tragedy was the straw that broke the camel's back.

Paddy's depression began with bouts of moodiness after the funeral. Moll knew the tell-tale signs and mentally prepared herself for several weeks of it. He fidgeted about the house in the evenings after work instead of going fishing. He started several little household jobs and didn't finish them. She sighed patiently while he patched the floors upstairs, stripped down the wallpaper in the hall, and painted part of the front door. Halfway through every little job he started, his interest waned. Moll was patient and understanding.

'The nerves take time to heal,' she said. But when he talked of breaking-up the yard and laying new concrete, she put her foot down.

'New concrete in the yard, how are you!' she exclaimed one morning, after he'd gone to work.

'What's that, Aunt Moll?' The Boy asked.

'Your Uncle Paddy wants to put down new concrete in the yard, and it only done two years ago. Dragging that bloody river had a terrible effect on him. He's after doing it once too often, that's what it is. That fecking work should be left to younger men who have the stomach for it. He's depressed and he won't go to the doctor for me.'

'He's not himself these days,' The Boy said glumly. 'There's a great rise of trout every evening and he won't go fishing when I ask him.'

'He's down in the dumps and he can't help himself at the minute,' Moll said, her voice getting soft again. 'Anyhow, you get yourself off to school now.' The Boy wondered why she put on her Sunday coat when it was only Wednesday.

'Where are you going, Aunt Moll?'

'I'm going to get the mountain to come to Mohammad,' she said and closed the door behind her. The Boy thought about it for a moment. Little ripples of bewilderment crossed his face and then he figured it out.

'She must be going to see The Doc,' he told himself. The Doc was a fisherman himself and a friend of the family.

Paddy stayed home from work for a long time after The Doc's visit. Three times a day, without fail, Moll measured out two level teaspoons of a greenish grey liquid from a medication bottle and stood over him while he swallowed it. Weeks slipped by and the combination of rest and the prescribed elixir began to work. Paddy abandoned his notion of concreting the yard, and instead turned to books and the creation of wonderful fishing flies. After school each day, The Boy joined him at the fly-tying table and learned how to make the most beautiful and intricate trout fly patterns. Paddy was a competent entomologist. He couldn't reel-off the obscure Latin classifications of insects – not many of them, anyway – but he identified the diverse groupings of aquatic insect by their shape, colour, behaviour, and habitat distribution.

Colour was at the heart of what The Boy learned from him about making fishing-flies. Paddy went to extraordinary lengths to ensure that the shade of the materials he used matched the natural hue of the insects that he wanted to imitate. He had an alchemist's approach to colour-matching, and used a variety of tools, methods and materials. He mixed elderberry and blackberry juices in varying proportions to stain raffia that would mirror the purple blue bodies of the Iron Blue Duns. He boiled rock lichens with Epsom salts and vinegar to reproduce the vivid yellow patterns of the Yellow Sallies and Yellow Partridges.

But sometimes the splendour of the colours came at a price, and The Boy was almost nauseated by the foul-smelling, obnoxious brew that his uncle concocted to dye hanks of white cock feathers and silk threads into the most wonderful shades of olive green and yellow-green. At a decent distance from Moll and the neighbours, Paddy created his fly-fishing masterpieces amidst the stench of boiling donkey urine and washing soda.

'If Paddy's flies were paintings, they'd be Rembrandts,' said James Wyse.

'And if they were violins, they be Stradivariuses,' said his brother Dave.

'Rembrandts and Stradivariuses,' nodded Simon Wyse.

After a few weeks, The Boy had mastered some of the mandatory skills of the fly-dresser and learned to make flies whose poetic names were as 'colourful' as the forms themselves. Every so often, he would reel them off in his mind, just to enjoy the sheer poetry of them. The Wickhams Fancy, Tupps Indispensable, the Peacock and Blae, and Greenwell's Glory. He loved most of all the magical patterns Paddy himself created, and the peculiar names he gave them.

He loved to say them out loud, and sometimes listen as the Three Wise Men repeated them in their wondrous, wondering voices.

'*Maggie Twomey's Bloomers*,' said Dave.

'*Never Let You Down*,' said James.

'Ah, *Me Lovely Yella Lady*,' sighed Simon.

'And what's *your* favourite, young fella?'

'*Bejasuswegotchya!*'

'A good choice, a good choice,' they chimed.

Moll and The Boy knew Paddy was getting over 'the nerves' when he began asking about the river again. What level is it at? Who's catching trout? What are they catching them on? But it was a slow recovery, and his enthusiasm ebbed and flowed. Moll decided she'd speed up his progress, as it were. She was determined to get him out of the house and back on the river again as soon as possible. 'For his own good and my own sanity,' she said. The plan which she devised to achieve these aims was devilish but simple. She was confident that it would grate at the very essence of Paddy's pride as a riverman.

It was Saturday morning. The Boy answered a knock on the door and found The Dalt standing all business-like and shooting questions.

'Is he there?'

'He is.'

'Good, 'cause I want to see him urgently. I have a few serious words to exchange with him, if you please,' and walked past, straight into the kitchen.

'Dalt, auld stock,' Paddy said, brightening. 'What brings you over here so early on a Saturday morning?'

'Well, you asked the question so I'll come straight to the point,' answered The Dalt, planting himself in the chair opposite Paddy.

'Were you ever any other way,' wondered Paddy.

'Paddy Whelan, I don't want to see that grand cot of yours falling into the wrong hands.'

'What are you talking about, Dalt?'

'I'll make you a decent offer on it now, this minute. And when it's in my keeping you'll have the peace of mind knowing that it will be looked after proper, the way you'd look after it yerself.' Paddy's eyes popped and he sat bolt upright in the armchair.

'Were you drinking, Dalt?'

'No, I wasn't. I just want to be the first one to get his speak in for that lovely cot, and of course, if you're getting rid of the fishing gear, I'd be interested in that too.'

'You're stark raving bonkers, Dalt. What makes you think that I'm selling the cot, or me fishing gear for that matter?'

'With all due respect to you now, Paddy, everyone is saying that you're finished with the river, that you're not able for it any more. And Dave Wyse was saying that you might never work again.'

'The Three Wyse Men!' Paddy breathed hard through his nose. 'I should have guessed they'd add two and two and get five!'

'I can tell you here and now, Paddy Whelan – if there's any misunderstanding, you can't blame the Wyse brothers, or myself for that matter. Everyone knows that you had a bad turn because Doc Callaghan himself was seen coming out of the house a few weeks ago. What's more, the cot is full up to the gunnels with water.' The Dalt paused and fixed him with an accusing stare. 'That's not your style Paddy Whelan, neglecting the cot like that.'

'Just because there's a little sup of water in the arse of the cot doesn't mean that I'm dying, or that I'm selling my grand cot either.' Paddy thumped his fist on the arm of the chair.

'Well, I'm surely delighted to hear that you're not dying,' said The Dalt. 'But the question is: *are* you selling the cot?'

'The cot is not for sale, and it never was,' Paddy growled, wagging a finger at The Dalt.

'All right, all right, Paddy. I get the message,' The Dalt said, half out of the chair and reaching for the door handle.

'Sit down, Dalt.'

'Thanks Paddy, I will.' The Dalt eased his angular form back into the chair and resumed the offensive. Paddy was rising to the bait.

'Do you know that there's one, maybe two, gigantic pike in the Back River and they're creating havoc with the ducks and the waterhens there? Heaven knows how many trout they're scoffing every day too.'

'Pike have to live too, Dalt, and contrary to common but mistaken belief they're a very important part of the river system.'

'There's only one good pike, Paddy Whelan, and that's a dead one!' The Dalt exclaimed.

'Jaysus, that's just typical Dalt. That's just the kind of deluded, blinkered thinking that I'm talking about. If you don't like it, don't want to eat it, or don't understand what purpose it serves in the overall scheme of things – kill it. That's just typical, Dalt.'

'Well then, Paddy, tell me this: what would *you* do with the pikes in the Back River?'

'Bring them somewhere else. To a deeper spot, a wider part of the main river where they wouldn't have such an easy time catching helpless water hens or ducks. Take them where they'd have to work hard for their dinner.'

'Sure it doesn't matter where you move the buggers – they're still going to eat trout.'

'Right, but the same pike must work a lot harder for their grub and they'll use up a lot more energy doing it. That means they get very shrewd very quickly and they start stalking the slower, weaker fish. When they get like that it helps the river along because they cull the diseased fish from it. Now, do you get my drift, Dalt?' Paddy looked smug and superior as he knocked the top of The Dalt's argument.

'Of course I do,' said The Dalt. 'But who's going to get rid of the bastards?'

'I am!' said Paddy.

'Well, I suppose that mean's the cot is definitely withdrawn from the market then?'

'It was never on it in the first place Dalt,' growled Paddy.

'That's settled so.' The Dalt handed Paddy a pack of Woodbines. 'My Mother always told me it was polite to bring gifts to the sick.'

'Good luck, Dalt, my auld stock, and thanks.'

'You're welcome. Sure the river just ain't the same without you,' The Dalt said, waggling his eyebrows at The Boy as he went.

On Sunday morning, when The Boy came downstairs for breakfast, the fishing bags and the rods were already lined-up at the hall
door. Moll was humming to herself in the scullery as she buttered
thick slices of bread for sandwiches. She layered them with slices of
ham and then spread mustard over them.

'When you have that breakfast scoffed up, Huck, go out and
get the gill net from the shed, will you?'

'OK, Uncle Paddy,' The Boy said. 'Are we going after those big
pike The Dalt talked about?'

'We are.'

Moll and The Boy exchanged glances.

'There's more than one way of skinning a cat,' she whispered.

Chapter 12

Old Pike Wisdom

'The Dalt was right, Huck,' Paddy said, surveying his cot. 'She's full to the gunnels. Get that big plastic bucket from under the hedge. We'll be here all day if we bail her out with tin cans.'

They set to work with the bucket and when the water was low enough they stepped on board and scooped out the remaining water with the bean tins. An hour passed before they were ready to push off onto the river.

'The nerves can play funny tricks with the auld mind, Huck.'

'All I know is that we're after missing loads of good fishing.'

Paddy nodded sagely and a little sadly.

'Only for your Aunt Moll and The Dalt, we might have missed a lot more of it.'

'He wound you up good and proper all right. Hopping mad, you were, when he asked about buying the cot.' The deep burnished gold of Paddy's laughter mingled with the silvery laughter of his nephew and danced out over the river.

'There I was, like a bad auld car battery, getting jump-started by The Dalt. You know, Huck, he acts like a tough man at times, but under that hard outer shell of his, he's really a decent auld sod. An uncut diamond, that's what our Dalt is – a rough, uncut diamond.'

'Whereabouts do you figure the big pike is, Uncle Paddy?'

'She's probably near the sluice gate at Dudley's Mill.'

'How do you know it's not a he?'

'I'm only guessing, Huck, but generally the females grow much larger than the males do. That's the way Mother Nature herself looks after things.'

'How do you know nature is a she and not a he?'

'I don't. That's just the common way of describing nature. Gentle and kind and nurturing, I suppose, like a mother.'

'Don't know about that, Uncle Paddy. What about the big hurricanes and tidal waves and volcanoes and earthquakes?'

'I'm a saint, that's what I am. A fecking saint. So what do you want to call her then?'

'Father Nature.'

'Fair enough then.' Paddy put on his 'big' voice. 'From this day forth I decree that Mother Nature is to be called Father Nature. Happy now?'

'I am, but what's a decree?'

'Will you get the net there, and the poles for staking it out because if I stay here answering your questions we'll never shift the pike! You pole her down, Huck. I'm just going to sit back here, take in the view and relax.'

The Boy poled the cot out and Paddy took a mouth organ from his pocket. His mood was flamboyant and he was more contented than he'd been for weeks. They sailed on down under the big chestnuts and past Malcolmson's house to the strains of 'China Doll' and 'The Moon Behind The Hill'. Swans were preening on the wall of the weir, and the plumage on the cygnets was changing from grey to adult white.

'There were six chicks there the last time I counted,' Paddy said, "and I'd bet a thousand pounds the bloody pike took the other three.'

'Would a pike eat birds as big as that, Uncle Paddy?'

'Not when they're the size they are now, Huck, but when the chicks are young and vulnerable. Big cannibal pike will eat just about anything they can get their big toothy jaws around.'

'How are we going to catch them?'

'Let's find them first and then you'll see how it's done.'

They began their search at the headwater of the Back River and worked their way along underneath the overhanging bushes on the Waterford shore. The sun was high in the sky and they could see the bottom of the river clearly. The Back River was a different world, sheltered from wind by the thick vegetation on both banks. It was an oasis – flat-calm and somehow mysterious. Dense growth mollified the water's rumble over the weir to a soothing pulsing sound that came and went on the whim of the breeze. In the higher reaches, the water moved at a snail's pace. Lower down near the mill, part of the dividing wall had been swept away by flood, and the Back River rushed through to team up with the main artery of the River Suir. On the near side of the gap, sand and silt piled up against the shore, shelving precipitously into a deep hole. The trough extended three hundred yards from the maw of the breach to a colossal black rock protruding from the river bottom.

Halfway along the gully they found two pike lying in the shadows. One was a small jack pike, the other a larger fish of about ten pounds weight. But these weren't the fish they were looking for. They were close to the Mill now, and they still hadn't located the large pike.

They poled up the opposite shore but it was very difficult to see the bottom there. In the deeps, it was almost impossible. Two hours of searching gave them an appetite, and they pulled ashore to brew up.

'Let's think like a pike would,' Paddy said, filling the billycan with water from the river.

'Food!' said The Boy.

'Yes, food could be the answer all right, or is it your own belly that you're thinking about?'

'Both!'

'A pike has three basic instincts. Like you, he's always thinking about his stomach. Then when he has the grub inside him, all that he wants to do is lie up and digest it. But if it's not safe to lie out in the open, what'll he do then, Huck?'

'He'll find a spot where he can hide.'

'Now you have it. So what we have to do now is find out if he's on the prowl, or fast asleep somewhere.'

The Boy gathered leaves and dry twigs and boiled the can. The tea was strong and sweet with a hint of smoke to the taste, and not a word was spoken as they made short work of the sandwiches. Paddy lighted a cigarette, drew in and expelled a plume of blue-grey smoke.

'If that pike is as big as I think he is, I reckon he's a night feeder.'

'How do you make that out.'

'Because predatory fish don't get to grow very big if they're stupid. If he's big, then he's cunning, and that means he feeds at the safest time, when it's dark.'

'So he'll lie up during the day?'

'Now you have it, Huck.'

'He could be snoozing at the big black rock. There's at least ten feet of water there.'

'You could be right, Huck, so this is what we'll do.'

The new plan of action was put in motion. Paddy poled the cot back up to the head of the Back River. The Boy climbed a tree on the island overhanging the black rock and settled himself into a good position. The floor of the gully was visible and he could see a good distance to his left and right.

'I'm in the crow's nest!'

'Right. I'll start then.'

The Boy felt a surge of excitement run through him. His lofty view of the river peeled away the glare off the water, and shafts of sunlight illuminated the riverbed. He watched a shoal of perch hunting minnows in and out of the lily stems. Several minnows fluttered on the surface, casualties of the feeding orgy below. The perch sensed their distress signals, swam up and devoured them. The wheels of a bicycle peeped through the mud on the edge of the lily pads, and he could make out the saddle-springs and a section of the iron basket.

The riverbed was a mixture of sand and shingle. He counted twenty fluke, freshwater flat fish, lying along the edge of the gravel bar. Dozens of black sargasso eels swam in and out of the gully, unflustered by the perch or the flat fish. It was like a natural larder, he thought. No wonder it was the favourite hunting ground of that old dog otter.

'Can you see any pike?' Paddy shouted from the cot.

'No – not even a small jack pike!'

'Right. You keep your eyes peeled and I'll stir up the bottom. If you see anything, shout. But make sure you watch where it goes.' He zig-zagged the river from bank to bank making as much noise as he could. He slapped the ribs, scraped his feet on the keel boards and slashed the surface with the paddle. Fish began to scurry away from every nook and cranny. They streaked from under the plants, darted out from deep-set roots, and appeared from the shadows of obscured ledges.

'Jesus, Uncle Paddy, there's fish all over the place,' The Boy shouted. 'Big trout as well. Some of them have taken off towards the Mill.'

'Any pike now, Huck?'

'Not a sign of a pike anywhere.'

'OK. Move down the bank a bit, and climb up that sycamore tree at the gap. Look out for any movements in or out of the hole there.'

Perched halfway up the sycamore, The Boy noted a mass of dense weed on his left. At the far shore, the sandbank sloped down dramatically into a deep hole of water. He could scarcely see the silhouette of a tree trunk wedged on the bottom. Several of the branches spiralled out from the trunk like broken umbrella spokes, and the rest were half-buried in the mud. It looked like a very large insect crawling along the riverbed. And then he saw it – a dark shape huddled underneath a bough.

'Uncle Paddy, I think I've found him – her, I mean. Come down quick and have a look.'

'Are you sure it's a pike?'

'I'm not certain, but it has the shape of a fish. It's lying beside a log on the bottom but if I can get higher up I might be able to see better.'

'Don't do anything for a while,' Paddy said. 'Let me drift down over it and have a look for meself.' There was a frenzy of activity when the shadow of the cot moved across the sunken tree trunk. Clouds of mud swirled up from the bottom and five or six small pike darted out of hiding.

'Holy divine, where did they come from in such a hurry?' gasped Paddy.

'They were under the log. I think the cot spooked them.'

'They must have been feeding on something down there. I'll take a look. You keep your eyes peeled and tell me if you see anything else from the crow's nest.'

'Will do, Captain.'

Paddy turned the boat broad-side and let it drift over the spot where the tree-trunk lay submerged. Then, he knelt on the keel boards, leaned over the side, and poked at the tree trunk with the tip of the pole. When the pole knocked against it, the dark shape flipped over to reveal the off-white belly of a fish. The Boy looked down and saw the unmistakable outline of a large tail and a bulky head.

'It's a fish all right,' he yelled down to Paddy.

'But a dead fish,' said Paddy. 'A very large dead fish, Huck. It's a pike. I can make out the shape of its head and I can see the dorsal fin. I'm going to anchor up here and see if I can snatch him off the bottom to have a better look. Stay up there and guide me along.' He made several attempts before he managed to move the fish from the deep water into a shallow area under the sycamore tree. By the time The Boy had climbed down, it was beached on dry land.

'That was a mighty fine fish in its day,' said Paddy, after surveying it in silence for a long moment.

'I never saw a pike as big as that before. Never.'

'An' it's unlikely you'll see one like it again for a long, long time, Huck. That pike was at least thirty five or forty pounds weight in its prime.' He looked at the fish closely, and swore under his breath.

'What kind of stupid bastards would shoot a beautiful fish like that?' he said, and for a moment his face was a mask of anger.

'Shoot it? What do you mean, shoot it? How do you know it was shot, Uncle Paddy?'

'Oh it was shot all right. Look – there's a bullet hole, and there's another.' He pushed his finger into holes in the decaying flesh.

'That's one fish we won't need to relocate into bigger water, Huck. And if my suspicions are confirmed, we won't have to move any more of them from this stretch either.'

They steered the cot for home. The swans had left the top of the weir and were feeding under the chestnuts on the Waterford bank. But The Boy hardly noticed them. He was angry because someone had shot the big pike.

'Why do people kill things like that, Uncle Paddy? I mean, just for the heck of it.'

'Several reasons Huck, but I think mainly from pure ignorance. Some people don't seem to understand that the balance of nature is finely tuned. Certain folk think they have a right to dispose of God's creatures simply because they don't like them, or because they get in their way. If they think that an animal is interfering with their sport or threatening their livelihood, they destroy it. Their attitude to wild life is all screwed up, out of keeping with nature's own plans.'

'But we were going to trap that pike and take it down the river where it would have plenty of space to live.'

'Yeah, I know. But you must understand that a lot of so-called anglers regard the pike as vermin. They don't see any place, or role for it in a river where there's salmon and trout. They have this strange-fangled idea that pike eat loads of fish, every day.'

'And they don't, do they?'

'Pike spend most of their day lazing about on the bottom. It takes them ages to digest a good meal. Half a pound of trout will keep a pike going for two or three days.'

'Even a huge pike like this one?'

'The older they get, the less active they are, and the less they feed. Instead of eating several small fish, they probably eat one big fish when they need it.'

'But, Uncle Paddy, if he's big then mustn't he eat more than the smaller fellas?'

'Well, let me put it like this, Huck,' Paddy said, a wise grin spread across his face. 'Who eats the biggest dinner at home – you or me?'

'Me,' The Boy said, without a moment's thought.

'Well, there you are then. You eat more because your body is growing and I eat less because I'm fully grown. Big pike get to be that way because they're clever. Large pike won't make eejits out of themselves chasing all over the river after more energetic fish. No, they'll wait under cover until a lazy or injured straggler passes by their lair, and then they'll pounce. You mightn't think it now, Huck, but auld age has some advantages, and one of them is wisdom.'

The Boy looked up at him and a big grin spread across his freckled face.

'You know a lot of wisdom, Uncle Paddy.'

Chapter 13

Great War and Little Duck

Dan Franey in the lodge always kept an eye on their bikes while Paddy and The Boy were fishing. They leaned them at his wrought iron gates, untied rods and net-handle from the cross-bar, and then pushed the machines out of sight under a privet hedge. Dan had been head gardener at the Big House, back in the days when the owners had enough money to lavish on such luxuries, and cultivated unusual succulents collected from every corner of the world.

'You mightn't think it now, Huck, but Dan Franey was known far and wide for his talents as a gardener,' Paddy said as he untied the rods and net-handle from the crossbar. 'He had a great gift for growing things that were out of the ordinary.'

Dan was equally respected as a breeder of gun dogs, and specialised in red setters and springer spaniels. The Boy often thought it odd that a man with such a great reputation for breeding hunting dogs never actually hunted himself. That evening, he was to find out why.

Dan heard the bikes rattling against the railings. He opened the door to investigate and greeted them with a gummy smile.

'Paddy Whelan! So it's yourself and the young fella that's in it.'

'Well, tell me now Dan, who were you expecting? I don't think royalty would arrive on two auld bone shakers like these,' laughed Paddy. 'Then maybe it was the President himself that you were waiting for?'

Dan laughed out loud and Paddy raised his voice to a merry octave.

'How are you, Dan? How's life treating you?'

'Fair to middling, Paddy. I'm still six feet over the ground so far. And by the way, if it was luminaries I was expecting, I'd have shaved and put out the red carpet.'

'Do you want a few trout if we get them, Dan?' Paddy knew Dan had a passion for fresh brown trout.

'I'd love a few Paddy, but for Christ's sake, won't you clean them out for me, otherwise they'll have to go on the pan, guts and all.'

'Grand. We'll drop in a couple on the way back so. That's if we get any, mind.'

While Paddy and Dan were talking, Wiggles made his way into the lodge and came out again with Dan's dogs in tow. One of them was an old red setter, very grey about the jowls, and the other was a frisky liver-and-white spaniel whose markings and behaviour made it remarkably similar to Wiggles. They could easily have been mistaken for brothers. The red setter, though old, was full of fun. She licked The Boy's hands and face, lavishing him with every ounce of affection she could muster, and then rolled over on her back to have her belly scratched.

Dan was once renowned for his pin-point accuracy with a gun. He'd been known as a fine sportsman, and one of the best shots in the country, especially when it came to shooting snipe. The Boy had heard several stories about his exploits in the Comeragh

Mountains, and how he would disappear into the hills for weeks on end, surviving on what he could trap and shoot.

The Boy grew more inquisitive with every tale. He wanted to know more and more about Dan's expertise with guns and good hunting dogs, but Paddy always dodged his questions. The Boy's curiosity built up and he could contain it no longer. The great question was like a river inside him about to burst its banks, and he had to ask. Bold as brass, he looked Dan straight in the eye.

'Mr Franey, why don't you go shooting with the dogs any-more?'

Paddy cut in straight away.

'I'm sorry Dan. I'm awful sorry about that. He was told not to broach that matter with you. He's far too nosey for his own good. Full of questions. It's his age I suppose.'

Paddy's words were like a two-edged sword; one edge of it blunted in apology, the other sharp with reprimand. He glared, and The Boy looked at him and saw an expression worse than Moll's the day Wiggles accidentally broke her favourite vase. He knew then that he'd stepped across the thin line between mere curiosity and unacceptable behaviour.

'Easy there, Paddy. Easy now. It's fine, so it is,' Dan said. 'Let me tell him all about it in the best way that I can. What I say may not satisfy but it might open his eyes a bit.' He reached for a large straw mat that covered the red terracotta tiles on the porch, and he pulled it towards them.

'Sit down there beside me now, lad,' he said, pointing to the mat. Paddy calmed down and leaned against a pillar on the porch. Dan reached into a pocket for his pack of cigarettes and they both lit up. The old man blew a smoke-ring, and stared at it till it drift-ed off and dissipated, before he spoke again.

'Well now, it's like this young fella. I used to love hunting with me dogs. In fact I liked nothing better than getting out of bed on a cold frosty winter morning and setting off up the mountain with a couple of greenhorn dogs at my heels. By God, I had some great hounds that time too. Tipsy — an Irish red setter, she was — had the spirit of a Celtic warrior and a nose on her like no other dog I ever had before, or since.'

His eyes glazed-over with pride and he took another deep drag on the cigarette before continuing.

'People gave me great credit for the fine dogs that I trained over the years. But let me put the record straight here and now. It was that particular setter that did all the work, not me.'

'What do you mean, Mr Franey?' said The Boy.

'She was a natural-born hunter, that's what I mean. Ready and willing to please me at the drop of a hat. What was even more astonishing, though, was the fact that she seemed to know what I wanted her to do before I ever asked her to do it.'

'How could she know that?'

'There are certain things we'll never fully understand, lad.' It was Paddy who answered. 'But what Dan is saying is perfectly true. I saw that dog in action myself and she was truly amazing. Do you remember that day when she brought the injured duckling up from the river and into her kennel, Dan?'

'I do, Paddy, as clear as day. She wouldn't let God nor man near that poor little thing for six long days and nights. Every time I think of it, I'm still dumbfounded by her antics. She actually saved the duck's life, so she did. Every time that I fed Tipsy she'd take bread out of her dish and bring it back to the kennel for the duck. After a few days, when the duck was getting her strength back, the poor little thing would try to make her way over to the dish. But no, Tipsy wouldn't have that at all and she'd nudge it back inside again like a mother hen fussing over her chicks. She had a great nature that dog.'

'What happened to the duck after that, Mr Franey – did it get better?' The Boy asked.

'It did. It got better all right. Well, in fashion, I suppose. She had a broken wing and a broken leg, but at least she survived – saved by a hunting dog! Now who'd ever believe that?'

'The dog and the duck remained the best of friends, Huck,' Paddy said. 'And they were always together except when the dog was up in the hills with Dan. In a way, it was very funny to watch them so it was. Picture it! A dog and a duck sitting at the gates of the lodge like the lord and lady of the manor waiting for the chauffeur to arrive. I had a little terrier at the time and when we arrived, without fail, that duck would attack if it went over to sniff Tipsy. It would kick up such an almighty racket that the terrier would run off with her tail between her legs. Is that the truth or not, Dan?'

'On my word of honour, lad, that's the truth and the whole truth, so help me God. But listen to this though. When your uncle Paddy there began to make his way down through the gardens towards the boat, the duck and Tipsy would follow on behind him as if they were out for an evening stroll together. The duck had a limp and it dragged one wing along the ground. Every couple of yards or so the dog would stop and take a look over its shoulder to see if the duck was trailing too far behind. If it was, the dog would sit down and wait for it to catch up with her. Oh, it was really priceless to watch them together.'

'When they reached the river the duck might, or might not, decide to have a little swim. Whenever it did go in, Tipsy sat down on the riverbank barking until it came safely ashore again,' Paddy added.

'Where's the dog and the duck now, Mr Franey?' The Boy asked.

'Dan, lad, call me Dan,' the old man gently chided.

'Where are the snows of last winter?' asked Paddy, rhetorically. 'You weren't even a glint in your mother's eye when all that happened. It was before Dan went off to France to fight in the Great War.'

'That terrible, idiotic war,' Dan said. 'Now let me see what I can tell you about that great foolishness.'

'Are you sure you're able for it, Dan?' Paddy was concerned. 'You don't have to upset yourself, remembering all that again.'

'Yarra, I can tell him what I can of it and if I get jittery I can stop. Can't I Huck?'

'Sure, Mr Franey – Dan. Sure you can.'

Dan stared straight ahead into empty space for a while and drew hard on his cigarette. He inhaled deep and then blew a long trail of wispy blue smoke into the air. His eyes were glazed over, his thoughts miles away.

'What d'ya know about the war, lad?' he asked gently.

'The First World War, is it?'

'Yes, the Great War. What are they teaching you in school about that, lad?'

'Nothing much. We do sums, English, Irish, and religion. Mostly religion though.'

'Holy divine God, do you mean to tell me that they learn you nothing about history, especially about the most important event that happened in the world for the last thousand years or more?'

'No. We sometimes do a bit of Irish history, but nothing about the big war.'

The smoke from the two cigarettes lingered like an acrid blue-grey lace curtain around the front of the lodge, and Dan gazed through it, back to the long-gone days.

'Now, let me think. Where should I begin? August 1914, I suppose, when the war broke out. Germany declared war on France and within a few days the whole of Europe was at each other's throats. All over Europe, in Canada, and Australia, thousands and thousands of young men were tripping over each other to sign up and fight. Some of these lads were only youths, not much older than yourself, who lied about their age so they could get into the army. Little did they know what awaited them on the battlefields in France.'

'Why?'

'Why what, lad?'

'Why did so many want to join up and fight?'

'Now that's a very hard one to explain. But at the time, people were convinced that the state was more important than anything else. *Dulce et decorum est, pro patria mori.*'

'What does that mean?'

'That's Latin, lad: "How sweet and fitting it is to die for one's country." That's what they drummed into young lads' heads, back then. We were brainwashed with that kind of shit for years before the war broke out, both at home and at school. So, when it happened every young man's head was filled up with the notion that there was no better way to prove his manliness than to sign up and be willing to die on the battle fields of France for nationalism.'

'Sure that was an awful thick way to be thinking,' said The Boy.

'Well, you're right there, my lad, because I certainly hadn't the full quota of sense on board when I packed my bags and sailed off to England to join up.'

'What age were you then?'

'What age was I? Well, England declared war on Germany on the third of August 1914, my birthday. I was born in 1890, so, go on then, use the sums they teach you in school. What age was I?'

'Twenty-four.'

'Good lad. And what age am I now, then?'

'Well it's 1961 now, so you're ... you're ... O holy God, Mr Franey – Dan, I mean – you're ancient so you are. You're seventy-one years old! Even Uncle Paddy's not that old, so he's not.'

The two men rocked back and forth with laughter.

'And what age are you, now?' Dan asked when he'd recovered from the attack of coughing that followed the outbreak of merriment.

'Well, I was born in 1950 – so you tell me,' The Boy said cheekily. Dan wrinkled his brow and affected complex mental arithmetic.

'Eleven!' He said after a minute or two. 'A mere nipper, that's all you are. I suppose you think that twenty-four was a bit ancient to join the army too.'

'Naw, twenty-four's not that old – certainly not as bad as seventy-one.'

'Anyway,' Dan settled back into his narrative. 'After a bit of training in England – and mind you, it was only a bit – we were shipped over to France. I was a fairly good shot then so I was sent to the front straight away, as a sniper, a sharp shooter, no less. A greenhorn, that's all I was, and they threw me straight into the middle of it. I didn't know whether to fight or to run. I didn't run, of course, but I was often sorry after that I didn't.'

'When exactly did you go to France?' The Boy was consciously nudging him into the heart of the story.

'November, it was. The last week in November. That was the first time I looked down the barrel of a gun and pointed it at another man. I'll never forget that. We were sent to Ypres – everyone called it 'Wipers' – not too far away from Calais. They had a big skirmish going on there since the beginning of that October, and they sent us in to reinforce the allied positions there.'

'Did you shoot anyone, Dan? Did you?'

'Ah, for Christ's sake, Huck,' Paddy cut in, 'don't ask the man things like that.'

Dan's eyes had a faraway look again as he reached into his pocket for another cigarette. His voice trembled ever so slightly when he spoke again, and his hands shook.

'At that stage in the war, I don't honestly know whether I did or not. What I did then was to take aim at a figure off in the distance, close me eyes and then pull the trigger. Anyway, I was only there a few weeks when I got shot in the shoulder and sent behind the lines to recover.'

The Boy imagined bands of gallant heroes, fearless, brave, and splendid in their khaki uniforms, mowing down the lines of enemy troops before them. He opened his mouth to ask another question, but a sharp glance from Paddy made him close it again. Dan was so wrapped in his narrative that he didn't notice.

'Getting shot in the shoulder was the best thing that could've happened to me young fella. It kept me out of harm's way for nearly four months. The shoulder didn't heal up as fast as it should have, because I got an infection in it that took ages to clear up. In the heel of the hunt, they sent me back to England to recover. I was back there at the end of December and I stayed there till the following April. And then, when I was better, where did the bastards send me?'

'Back to France!' The Boy cried excitedly.

'Straight back to France. Back to Wipers and into the hell of another big scrap. The Germans were making a big push to try and oust the allies from their trenches and it was the first time that they used gas. Chlorine gas. It would creep over the ground like a yellow fog and burn the shagging eyes out of you.

'It'd catch you in the chest, too, so you could hardly breathe and it would leave a chap a respiratory cripple for evermore if he sucked in enough of it. It was worse at night because you couldn't see the bitch coming. And if you didn't get your gas mask on quick enough, you were shagged.'

He stopped and broke into a harsh, mirthless laugh.

'Sometimes, the wind changed direction so the bastards who'd released it got a dose of their own medicine when it carried back over their own trenches. Luckily, I never swallowed a lot of it, but I knew lads that suffered a terrible end from it. That was something I could never forgive the Germans for, bringing that into the war. I always think it was devilishly cowardly, not the way to fight. Anyway, I was a wiser man that time around, and I kept my head down as much as I could. That particular skirmish was short enough lived and after that I was sent up and down the front lines at the whim of the top nobs. They usually sent for me when they needed a sharp shooter, someone to do their dirty work for them. I'm not proud of it today, but I took out a good few Prussians with me rifle. At that stage I was as tough as the steel in the cannons and as rank as the grub they used to feed us. It was either them or me.

'Now young fella, don't get me wrong. Just because I was tough doesn't mean that I wasn't frightened. I was. When the German shells started whizzing over my head and dropping only yards away, or the machine gunners opened up – rat-a-tat, rat-a-tat – Christ lad,

I could never describe to you how frightened I was. I just curled-up in case anyone heard my soul screaming. I remember thinking: enough is enough, no more, just fuck off and let me die.'

Dan pressed his palms against his head and held them there like a gnarled vice. He swayed a little and trembled, and Paddy moved towards him, but he regained his equilibrium and drew in from the cigarette. It seemed an age before he spoke again.

'On more than one occasion, I pissed in me pants and for good measure I often shit meself as well. Well lad, that's how I carried on until the end of December 1915. Up and down the trenches day and night, week after endless shagging week. One bloody awful shindig after another. Then, out of the blue one day, not long before Christmas, the commanding Officer sent for me. I was told to drop back behind the lines and see the duty officer at operations HQ. Well, says I to meself, this is it, they have a right dirty job they want done so they call on Dan Franey to do it.

'The Command Post was about two or three miles behind the action and on my way there, I made my mind made up that whatever crap they wanted me to get involved in, I'd refuse point blank. I knew that disobeying orders would mean a court-martial, but I was gone beyond care. I saw it as a way out. Well, lo and behold, when I got there, one of the top-notch officers sat me down in his dugout and poured me out a brandy in his own tin mug.

'"Private Paddy",' said he, '"it's come to our attention that you're a top-notch shot, by Jove".'

'"Private Dan's the name Sir",' said I, "and I'm only a mediocre shot compared to some of the other lads out there fighting. There's one or two of them could shoot a fly off the top of a needle at five hundred yards", I said, doing my best to get out of whatever job he had lined up for me.

"'I say', said he, 'but you're far too modest, my good man. Our intelligence tells me that you're the best there is".'

"'Maybe", said I, "when I'm up in the Comeragh Mountains at home where there's none of them bastards out there trying to shoot the fucking head off me or blow the legs from under me".'

"'Well then, by Jove, if that's the truth soldier, you may not be the man that we require for the job after all", said he, stroking his big moustache with his fingers. "It's a crying shame, really, soldier, it really and truly is", he said, with a big smile spreading all over his chops. "We were convinced that you were the best man to return home to England and train our new crack squad of shooters".'

"'England? Train men to shoot?" said I, realising that I'd almost talked myself out of the chance I'd been praying for. "Sir, if I may, sir", said I, "it's possible that I was a touch modest there, sir. On occasions I've been known to shoot a fly off the top of a needle at seven hundred yards. And then sir, for good measure, I knocks the needle over with the ricochet, sir".'

"'You're a very lucky man, sergeant", he said. "Sergeant?" asked I. "Yes, sergeant", said he, pouring another brandy into the tin mug. "You leave on the next available transport. Good luck, soldier, and God speed".'

"'That night was one of the happiest nights of my entire life. I got drunker than drunk. A week later I was back in England with ten days R and R before I started training the new squad."'

'God,' The Boy gasped. 'You must've been delighted to get away from all that shooting and shelling. Did you come home to Ireland then when you had the training finished?'

'No such luck lad. I was training that bunch of fellas how to shoot straight from the end of January 1916 until the first week in July. Little did I know but my worst nightmare was about to begin.'

'Don't tell me, Mr Franey, I mean, Dan. They sent you back to fight again, didn't they?'

Dan rubbed his forehead and reached into his pocket for another cigarette.

'The Somme lad. They sent me to the Somme. The greatest hell-hole that God or Satan ever created on this earth. Day and night, hour after hour, the shells and the shot kept raining down. There were bodies falling all over the place, dropping around me like flies, they were. Both sides were throwing everything they had at each other.'

He stopped and rapped his left thigh hard with his knuckles.

'I lost this at the Somme,' he said. The hollow sound echoed through the air around his words, and The Boy's mouth fell open, but no sound came out. He'd thought Dan's limp was just that: a limp, a consequence of old age and nothing more.

'A modern war they called it,' Dan picked up again. 'We had tanks and machine guns and planes up in the air, but the stupid bastards that were in charge made us scrap with the enemy like we were fighting with spears and bows and arrows. They marched us out across open ground straight into the pulverising teeth of the machine guns and the cannon. We were ripped to smithereens, massacred, cut down like pigeons at a shoot. No chance at all. No cover.'

For a time silence reigned, and Dan looked away into the trees. When he spoke again he was angry.

'Jasus Christ, when I think about it now, our so-called commanders, tucked up in their nice little billets miles behind the front lines had a lot to answer for. The smell of burning flesh. Well, now that's something I'll never get out of my nostrils. Or the screams of agony from the young fellas lying out there in no-man's-land, their life's blood turning the ground crimson.' The Boy stared into the distance, lost in the words.

'They were often out there for days waiting for help that very often didn't come. It was pitiful. Then the cries got fainter and fainter until they stopped calling altogether. I still wake up at night dreaming about that. Christ Almighty, what was it all for? What the fuck was it all about? That's what I want to know.'

The pack of cigarettes fell from his grasp onto the veranda. The Boy bent down to pick it up and saw the beads on his face. Paddy knew that Dan had had enough.

'There's no need to say any more, Dan,' he said. 'It took great courage to say what you did. But enough is enough. You've put yourself through enough.'

Dan's narrative had left him as spent as an athlete who'd just breasted the finishing tape and it took him a while to recover.

'I haven't talked about it so much for years,' he said wearily. 'Maybe I needed to. But young lad' – he pointed a boney finger at The Boy – 'I hope that what I've told you today will make you think twice about joining the army – any fucking army. Don't even think about joining up, promise me that.'

'I promise, Mr Franey, I promise.'

'There's no future in it, boy. I went off to do my patriotic duty and fight someone else's stupid fucking war. *Dulce et decorum est, pro patria mori*, and all that stuff. When I came back, I was a nervous wreck, shell shocked and bitter with the world.' Dan rubbed his hands together and looked directly at The Boy.

'The dog Tipsy was gone. My brother Mick told me she died from a broken heart. He said that when I left for the war the dog and the duck sat at that front gate every day for hours on end waiting for me to come home. After six weeks or so the dog stopped eating altogether and just faded away. He didn't know what happened to the poor auld duck. She just disappeared when the dog snuffed it and she never came back again.

'Anyway, young fella, you wanted to know why I don't go shooting with my dogs any more. Well, it's as simple as this. When I came back I was an entirely different man to the one you see before you now. I was a broken man, minus a leg, bitter with the world and very confused. There was no Tipsy waiting here for me to bring her off hunting. But that wasn't the worst of it. Whenever I tried to hold a gun I started to shake all over.

'My heart wasn't in the shooting anymore, and never was again. I carried on breeding dogs though, for years. Mick used to take them away for hill training. But when Mick passed on, that was it. No more dog-breeding. So now, that's it, my life story. There you are and there you have it.'

'Thanks very much for telling me. It was great to have a dog and a duck like them fellas, even for a short while, wasn't it, Dan?'

'It sure was, young fella. It sure was.'

Chapter 14

Man Overboard

Paddy and The Boy left the lodge and followed the rough path that trailed its way through mature woodlands down to the river. Dry twigs snapped under their feet and startled the wood pigeons in the monkey-puzzles. Fairy-caps and brown toadstools crushed by their boots retaliated with an angry pungent smell. A rabbit bolted from a grove of rhododendrons inside the high boundary wall of the estate. Wiggles took off in hot pursuit, chased it into a burrow at the base of an ash tree and came back panting, wagging its tail for approval.

Light streaming down through the branches seemed to be in love with the remains of an old summer house. Ivy and honeysuckle crawled in and out through the window frames unhindered, tumbling down in lazy clumps from the crumbling eaves. The yellow and pink roses were in full bloom around the front porch, as though unable to forget the summer house in its glory, but they were knotted and twisted, gone wild, and in danger of choking each other. Behind the summer house a long, tall hedge of pink and purple fuchsias played host to a swarm of bees whose hum-drumming cast a lazy tarpaulin over every other sound in the grove.

Scent from the roses and the honeysuckle joined forces to

dominate the more earthy smells of dead leaves and pine needles. The Boy's senses reeled from the passion of their perfume. He looked through a window and saw a rusty tilley lamp dangling from the rafters, and on the back wall, as though the tilley light were still on it, he could see quite clearly an old sepia photograph in its tarnished gilt frame. The four young men in the back row were wearing white shirts and pants, and the ladies, skirts that flowed down to their ankles. In front of them, on the grass, two large silver trophies glistened in the light, between them a pair of crossed tennis rackets. At the outside left of the front row, an elderly gentleman with big handlebar moustaches relaxed in a rattan chair stroking the head of a great Irish wolfhound. The pugnacious-looking bulldog at his feet looked as though at any moment he'd escape the constraints of the photograph and give chase, and The Boy detached himself from the window.

The mooring under the knurled chestnut was a good one, but it had certain disadvantages too. Twigs and fallen leaves had to be cleared, and bird-droppings washed off.

'Do you know what, Huck?'

'What, Uncle Paddy?' The Boy paused with a bunch of whispery leaves in his hand.

'Apart from been born downright cheeky, you must have been gifted with very special charms. As long as I know Dan Franey, I never heard him opening up like that before. And even though you disobeyed me, I'm glad in a way because it was a real eye opener for me too.'

'I thought you knew all about him.' The Boy was surprised.

'Oh, I knew he went through a rough time of it out there in France, all right, but I had no idea of the full extent of it. All that I ever got out of him were jokes about his wooden leg. I remember one time when he caught me looking at him limping he asked me did I want to know how he looked after it. I said I did – just to be polite, of course – and he said he oiled it three times every day and four times on Sundays, and once a month he went to the doctor for injections against woodworm and dry rot. I got a great laugh from that, but I realised he was telling me to mind my own business, too. I was amazed that he told you so much about himself.'

'Who looks after him now?'

'He depends a lot on the kindness of his friends and neighbours. They do his bit of shopping for him, clean up the house, give him a lift into town, and things like that. He loves fresh bread and I bring him a fresh grinder pan straight from the oven in the bakery whenever I can.'

Paddy tackled up the fly rod while his nephew finished bailing the cot. Wiggles lost his patience. He jumped aboard before the keel boards were back in place and took up watch at the bow. It was the last day of August and the river was alive with insects pockmarking the surface like raindrops. Lively music from the circus in the Horse Show grounds wafted across the fields. The ringmaster's voice was thin in the distance, the laughter muffled. The old dog otter sat on a ledge directly opposite with a very large eel in its mouth and they stopped to study his antics. At first glance, it seemed the eel was too slippery and he let it go down the bank and into the river. The otter waited for a long moment, then almost casually slipped into the water and captured it again. When the eel was firmly in his grasp once more he rolled over on his back and draped it across his belly triumphantly. They watched him repeat the performance twice more, playing with his catch like a cat plays with a mouse.

At the butt of Malcolmson's wall a pocket of trout was feeding away steadily. Some of them were hefty fish and they sucked down the flies with loud slurping sounds that betrayed their hunger. Paddy was confident they would take an artificial fly with equal determination. But first they'd have to get behind the fish, and that meant negotiating the thick weed-beds and their long trailing fronds of white flowers. There was just two ways they could cover the fish properly.

'What do you think we should do, Huck?'

'We could slip over to the opposite shore – there was good cover from the trees. Or we could pole out to the middle of the river.'

'My thoughts exactly,' agreed Paddy. 'Which option should we take?'

'Pole out to midriver,' said The Boy without a moment's hesitation. 'We don't want to get snagged on overhanging branches.'

'Fair enough. We'll do that, so.'

The Boy let the cot drift back a few yards, then started poling.

'Slowly now,' Paddy said. 'Don't be in any hurry. Take your time and when the nose is directly opposite that broken down fence, hold her there.'

The Boy was already an expert at holding the cot and easily kept the nose into the current, steady and straight. The task demanded fine technique more than physical strength. It was difficult at the beginning but he soon learnt it. The boat is stabilised before pushing the base of the pole firmly onto the river-bed. The pole is tilted at an angle of about thirty degrees. One hand is placed above the other. Body weight is transferred to one side of the boat and varying pressures are applied to the pole in order to counteract the flow of the river and the constant gyrations of the bow. Now he made it look easy. He poled with an easy smile and natural rhythm and lined the cot up with the broken fence. Then the easy smile became a little harder to hold and he struggled to keep the cot from drifting.

'This is tough work – hard spot to hold, Uncle Paddy,' he gasped. 'The pole is inclined to slip on the gravel and there's not much of it left over the water for me to lean on.'

'Do what you can, Huck. All I need is a few casts.'

The Boy struggled for a while and then managed to hold the cot's nose into the flow and keep it steady. His thoughts rambled away from what he was doing back to Dan Franey and what he had said earlier that evening. He thought about wounded soldiers bleeding to death on the battlefields of France. Was it shrapnel or a bullet that got Dan? How many Germans did he shoot?

'Will you hold the nose straight, for God's sake!' Paddy's roar brought him back to reality.

'Sorry, I was thinking about Dan.'

'Think about what you're doing! I'm trying to cover a great trout over there.'

'All right. Sorry,' The Boy apologised, but his mind wandered back to France once more.

'Nose me in a bit, will you?' Paddy said. 'She's drifting out of line again.'

'What?'

'Will you for heaven's sake push in the nose and watch what you're doing?'

'Sorry, Paddy.'

But the currents of his imagination were too powerful and his mind drifted away again. When he tried to swing the nose back, his right hand slipped from the pole and he tumbled head over heels into the river. He felt himself falling towards the bottom, his ears popping as he drifted down. Light scattered through the water and fractured the images above him. He saw Dan in the trenches, cannons blazing, guns spitting. He felt heavy. Couldn't breathe. Couldn't swim, never learned how. Christ! His lungs were ready to explode but he was still holding his breath. What was it his legs touched? Something solid. He heard a voice but he wasn't frightened. He was angry and pushed hard. The light grew brighter. There was a picture of an overboard canoeist in a magazine. He saw it again, and the instructions. Left hand over, catch the far gunnel. Right hand up, grab the near gunnel. Pull and slide aboard. The light was intense, the voice stronger, there was a shadow above him. He kicked hard and catapulted himself upwards. Surfaced. Grabbed with his left hand, snatched with his right. Sucked in so much air the clouds came down to meet him.

'Are you all right, did you hurt yourself?' Paddy said, grabbing the paddle.

'No, but get me ashore fast. I'm going home. I'm wet.'

Paddy nodded and paddled for the mooring. The Boy grasped the seat so hard his knuckles turned white. Halfway there he remembered that he'd seen the picture of the canoeist at the Boy Scout's hall, in a book called *Canoeing with Confidence*. The chapter called 'Getting Back In' said not to panic. Hold your nose while you're under the water. Stay with your canoe. Blow the whistle attached to your life jacket to draw attention to yourself when you surface.

'What fucking whistle?' The Boy muttered. 'What shagging life jacket?'

Paddy shook his head and poled faster.

'Home!' he said abruptly when they docked. 'Change your clothes and get back down here inside the hour!'

'No, I won't!'

'You heard me – an hour!' Paddy pointed to the lodge. 'Go, get your bike.'

'I won't. I'm too cold.' Fear as well as cold began to bite.

'Do as you're told – it's for your own good. Get up on that shagging bike right now. Go straight home, change your clothes and come back here straight away. Do you hear me? Go!'

The Boy's face crumbled and bitter tears ran down his cheeks.

'I hate you!' he cried. 'You're horrible, so you are!'

'Within the hour!' commanded Paddy. 'We have a big trout to catch before the light goes.'

By the time he made it up to the lodge, his thighs were raw from the wet trousers rubbing against them. Dan's red setter was sitting on the porch. She came over to investigate and sniffed at the trousers.

'Yeah, I'm sopping wet and what about it anyway?' he yelled, but straight away felt sorry and patted her on the head.

'It's not your fault girl, sorry,' he told her. 'It's Uncle Paddy's fault.'

Harsh cold air cut through his wet clothing as he cycled home.

'Everyone is staring at me,' he told himself, putting his head down and cycling harder. He had a one-way conversation with the bicycle as he rushed along.

'Uncle Paddy has no heart at all. Dammit, I nearly drowned, snuffed it, kicked the bucket, cashed my chips, and ended up in fucking Davy Jones' locker. And what does he want me to do? Go back and go out in that cot again after I nearly died. Jesus, he has no feelings at all!'

People walking along Duckett Street gazed in amazement at the sight of a dripping-wet boy cursing and swearing as he clattered along on a bicycle. They stared with their mouths open like gold-fish.

'Mind your own fucking business,' he muttered, making sure they wouldn't hear. When he got home he threw the bike against the wall and ran in through the doorway.

'Auntie Moll, Aunt Moll,' his voice came in a rush. 'I fell into the river and Uncle Paddy said I have to get back down and get into that fecking boat again. I nearly drowned, so I did. The only thing that saved my life was a picture in my head.'

He stopped and looked around in surprise.

'Aunt Moll, Aunt Moll! Where are you, Aunt Moll?' he cried. 'I fell in the river and a picture I saw in the Scouts hall saved me. Aunt Moll, do you hear me? – I fell in the river –'

He broke off and realisation dawned that the house was empty. Then he remembered. It was card night. Moll was away in some-one else's house playing cards. He ran out of swear-words and tried to invent new ones, then stripped naked where he stood. He left his wet clothes in a heap on the kitchen floor and ran upstairs to dress.

Paddy was anchored a few yards out from the bank, puffing on a cigarette.

'Are you all right in yourself now?' he asked, a kindly note in his voice.

'I think so, but I'm not going out in that boat again. I'll sit here and watch you,' The Boy said, half-sobbing. Paddy raised anchor and poled ashore. His voice and his face were very serious.

'You must have knocked your head against the gunnel when you went over that time.'

'No, I didn't get thumped at all. I just went straight in head over heels, splosh, like a big walrus, splash, straight in, no style at all.'

'Well, I'm convinced you hit your head.'

'Why do you think that?'

'Because there's a trout over there beside that bunch of reeds and he's about three pounds weight.'

'Why don't you have a go at him so?'

'The rod is waiting there in the bow for you. It's your turn to fish, Huck. Fair is fair. And that trout is waiting.'

'What happens if I fall in again, Uncle Paddy?'

'Lightning never strikes twice in the one place.'

And it didn't. When the light withdrew into the western sky the River Suir cloaked herself in a new identity and looked delicate and mysterious slinking off into the twilight. The clouds were bundled up behind the hills on the Waterford bank, promising rain that never came. In the half-light the colours were particularly intense. Beautiful dark shades of purple and magenta lurked in every shadow beneath the trees. The light in the western sky danced across the river onto the Tipperary shore, trailing plumes of saffron behind it. Layer upon layer the river soaked up the last beams of light from the west or borrowed it from the first stars flickering in the blue-purple sky.

'There he is, Huck!' Paddy pointed excitedly as the trout rose twice in quick succession under the far bank.

'I see him,' The Boy said, but the excitement in his voice was matched by a quiver of fear. 'But I'll fall in again when I'm casting. He looks well out of my reach.'

'You won't fall in,' Paddy reassured him earnestly. 'There's not a hope of that in the wide earthly world because I'll pole over near him and you won't have to stretch yourself at all, not even the least little bit.'

The Boy nodded uncertainly, and when the cot moved out he grabbed the edge of the seat and his fingers turned white again. His head spun and he began to sweat. Fear gnawed at the pit of his stomach.

'You're doing fine, Huck, just fine. Now pick up the rod beside you there and get ready to cast.'

'Ah, I don't know, Uncle Paddy. I'm a bit shaky. Maybe you should cover him.'

'You'll be just grand, so you will. Just have a go and let me hold the cot steady for you.' The Boy took up the rod and began stripping the line from the reel, but his hands were shaking so much the line wrapped around the tip of the rod and tangled up, and he swore aloud.

'Easy there, now,' Paddy said, gently.

'Look straight at the trout and the fly will land where you want it.' The Boy concentrated hard and then released the line, but the fly fell behind the trout.

'That trout'll never see it there.'

'Don't worry. Take another shot at it,' Paddy said encouragingly. 'You'll get over him this time.' The Boy nodded and began to lift the fly from the water for another cast. The trout saw the movement on the surface, swirled round, and snapped at it violently. The take was so hard and positive he felt the pressure of the fish immediately.

'Strike!" Paddy roared. But there was no need to set the hook. The fish had taken the fly with such determination it had hooked itself. The line screamed from the reel and the adrenaline pumped.

The Boy was shaking all over, but from excitement now, not fear.

'What weight do you think is in him, Huck?' Paddy asked, as the trout lay on the deck for Wiggles to lick it.

'About a pound and a half, pound and three-quarters maybe?'

'More like two and three quarters.'

'He's a good fish all right, but I don't think he's over two pounds.'

'I'll bet you a shilling that he's at least two and three-quarter pounds weight.'

'It's a bet, so. But if you win you'll have to give me the money so I can pay you.'

'I'm glad to see that you haven't lost your sense of humour. If that wetting did nothing else, it livened up your brain.' They both laughed, then Paddy stopped in the middle of it all and looked him straight in the eye.

'And by the way,' he said, 'how are you feeling now? Is the fear gone?'

'I – I think so.'

'Good lad. We'd better head back then. Do you fancy poling her back?'

'Yeah. I do but if you paddle as well, we'll get back faster and then we'll be in time to get chips on the way home.'

'Do you know what, Huck?' Paddy grinned as he set to work with the paddle.

'What, Uncle Paddy?'

'That soaking made you awful brazen, too.'

Chapter 15

The Last Soldier

'Well, did you catch me the supper?' Dan Franey was waiting with his dogs at the mooring when they pushed in. Wiggles jumped ashore the moment the cot nosed dry land and all three dogs scampered off together hunting in the grove.

'We got one good fish, Dan,' Paddy said, 'but I'm afraid you can't have it –'

'Oh, I see.' Dan was disappointed.

' – unless you happen to have an accurate weighing scales in the house.'

'Oh, it's like that is it? A dispute over the weight.'

'It's a bet, Mr Franey, not a dispute,' The Boy said.

'Let me see the fish and I'll be the judge, then.'

'No, no. We have to weigh him properly on scales. He's the biggest trout I ever caught. And what's more, I got a terrible wetting before I got it.'

'Sweet Jesus, but that's the biggest pike I ever saw in me entire life!' Dan exclaimed as Paddy held the trout up by the tail.

'Ah, Mr Franey,' The Boy said, sounding disappointed. 'I thought you knew more about fish than that. It's a trout, so it is. A brown trout."

'Oh! Forgive my black ignorance.' Dan winked across at Paddy. 'Now that I get a better look at him, I can see that you're right, of course. It's a trout all right. And I'm Dan.'

'Sorry, Mr Franey, – I mean, Dan. What weight do you think is in him?'

'Let me see now.' Dan dangled the fish in the crook of his index finger and held it at arm's length. Then he moved his arm up and down to judge the weight.

'Well?' The Boy asked impatiently. 'What's in him?'

'Easy now, lad, easy. You can't rush a delicate operation like this. It's a mighty difficult job for a man of my inexperience to get it right, a man who never judged the weight of a fish in his entire life.' The wink at Paddy was followed by a big toothless grin.

'He's three-quarters of a pound and not an ounce more.'

'Ah, Mr Franey – Dan – you're pure useless, so you are.'

'Maybe it's a teeny bit more. Only maybe mind you, for it could be the shell-shock talking.'

'Ah, Mr Franey, you're an awful chancer.'

'Come on then, we'll weigh it above in the lodge. I have good scales somewhere in the kitchen. I'll put the kettle on, so follow me up when you're ready.'

'Grand, Dan. That'll be grand,' Paddy said. 'A nice cup of tea would go down very well right now.'

They hid pole and paddle inside a disused pipe that ran underneath the garden wall. The Boy busied himself with the fishing gear, secured the cot, and tied up rod and net with old bootlace. When he looked up again, Paddy was standing motionless beside the estate wall.

'Are you feeling sick, Uncle Paddy?'

'I'm grand, Huck, grand, but listen,' Paddy said, earnestly gripping the lad's arm, 'listen to the otter going at it. I haven't heard him kicking up a rumpus like that before.'

'Is there something wrong with him? Is he hurt?'

'I don't know, Huck. He could be trying to keep another otter away from his territory by making as much noise as possible. He's a cute auld dog and knows he'd come out at the wrong end in a fight with a younger one, so he'll use his cunning instead.'

'Will we push off again and see what's up with him?'

'No Huck, it's too dark now, we wouldn't see anything out there.'

The three dogs came back panting, and stank of clay and damp leaves after their hunt in the woods. Wiggles had a twig stuck in his fur and whinged bitterly when The Boy bent down to remove it.

'Wiggles, what's up? You're a real auld softie, moaning over a bit of twig in your fur.'

'He's getting on in years, Huck, that's all — pushing on over the hill, like myself,' Paddy laughed. 'Come on, let's make tracks for the lodge. Dan'll be waiting.'

'God bless all here have you the tea wet.' Paddy ran all the words together in one breath. Dan was sitting at the far end of a sturdy pine table on which he had laid out three mugs and three plates. In the centre of the table, a brass lamp stood lighted, and next to it, a leather-bound photograph album. The lampshade was decorated with woodcock and snipe and its lower trim had a series of pictures depicting different stages of a shooting party: the hunters setting out on their quest, the chase, the kill, the fires lighting at dusk to cook the game. The brass was shining just as bright as the light from the globe. There was no other source of light, yet it bathed every inch of the room in a soft warm glow, giving the album's leather an opulent look, and enriching its silver lock and hinges.

'I have the kettle on,' Dan said, getting up from his chair. 'There's a nice bit of ham in the press, and to go with it, some lovely pickle that I got in Sparrow and Simpson. Oh, I nearly forgot, for the man who caught the pike for me – sorry, excuse my ignorance once again, the trout of course – there's lemonade and chocolate for after the supper.'

'Thanks, Mr Franey.' The Boy rubbed his hands together in delight. 'They're my favourites.'

Dan placed a steaming pot of tea and a plate of ham on the table.

'Dig in,' he said. 'Help yourselves because I won't play mother to you. I know that look in your eyes, lad, but there'll be no sweets till you've eaten something with a bit of substance in it.'

'I like ham as well, Dan.'

Paddy poured the tea while Dan buttered the bread. A flurry of hands descended on the bread and pickles and they ate in silence, punctuated by the click-clacking of knives and forks on Dan Franey's willow-pattern plates.

'Have another cup of tea to finish off, Paddy.' Dan rose from the table and walked across the kitchen to the dresser. 'I'll liven it up for you with a drop of "holy water".'

'Easy, Dan, easy,' Paddy urged as Dan poured.

'It's strictly for medicinal purposes, of course.'

'Oh, well, in that case,' Paddy grinned and lifted his mug. '*Slainte!*'

Dan gave a satisfied smile and turned his attention to The Boy.

'Go over there to that press, young lad, and on the top right-hand shelf you'll find what you're looking for. There's red lemonade, white lemonade and orange squash to choose from, but you have no choice at all with the chocolate. Plain only available today I'm afraid.'

'Plain's my favourite!'

'Any chocolate's your favourite, if you ask me.' Paddy chuckled.

Dan opened the photograph album and his finger fell on a page with a faded sepia photograph. It was of a group of soldiers lined up outside a large tent. They were waving flags, throwing their hats in the air, and making funny faces for the camera. One of the soldiers had a Union Jack draped over his shoulders.

'Who do you think that chap is?' Dan's craggy finger pointed to the young man with the flag. The Boy looked from Dan to the photograph and back again, and his eyes widened.

'Yeah, you're spot on. That's young Dan Franey there, the very same auld Dan that you see standing before you now.'

'God Mr Franey – Dan – you look like a real soldier in that photograph, so you do.' The old man smiled and rested his hand on the lad's shoulder and whispered loudly in his ear.

'But I *was* a real soldier.'

'Ah, I know that, but it didn't sink in fully till I looked at the photograph and saw all the other soldiers standing there with you.'

'Yeah, a picture like that can bring a story to life, I suppose.'

'Sure does, Mr Franey.'

'Mr Franey. Mr Franey! Anyone that can eat ham and chocolate like you can is entitled to call me Dan. So for the last time, it's Dan. If you were out in France we'd have sent you over to infiltrate the German side, do you know that?'

'Why?'

'Because you'd have eaten them out of house and home, so you would, and they'd have had no choice but to surrender with the starvation.'

'You're right there, Dan,' Paddy said. 'You couldn't have said a truer word. He has an appetite that could put any grown man to shame.'

'And God bless it, too,' said Dan. 'Now let me see, that particular photograph was taken the day before the first big fisticuffs at Wipers got under way. Most of the lads in the picture had already seen tough action at the battle of the Marne.'

'Were you fighting with them at Marne, Dan?'

'No. I arrived in France in November. Those lads had gone out there a few months before me. But yeah, I soldiered with them all at one time or another. That chap in the front row there: Sullivan he was, from County Mayo. "Shovel" Sullivan we used to call him because he could dig a hole faster and deeper than any other man in the whole bloody army could. When an order came for us to dig in, he used to say, "if it's a hole you want, it's a hole you'll get, and if you want me you'll find me at the other end of it back in Mayo".' Dan smiled to himself, and shook his head. 'The two lads standing beside Sullivan there, with their fists in the air, were two brothers from west Cork – Tommy and Finbarr Danagher. They were great comedians, always pulling someone's leg or planning some stunt or other.'

'Did you all fight together at the battle of Wipers, Dan?' The Boy asked.

'We did.' Dan reached into his pocket for a cigarette. 'Yeah, we did all right and only three men in that photograph survived the battle. Myself, Tommy Danagher, and that chap there, sticking his tongue out at the camera. Tommy got a chunk of shrapnel in the chest, but by some miracle he survived it. He suffered like hell though because he was left for dead on the battlefield. It was part of the miracle, I suppose, that two lads making their way back to our lines saw him twitching on the ground and dragged him back to our trenches.'

'Did they send him back home?'

'Yes they did, lad, eventually they did. He was so badly wounded it was months before they could transport him back to England
for proper treatment.'

'Did they send him back to France when he got better, like
they did with you, Dan?'

'No, the shrapnel that hit Tommy pierced one of his lungs and
it left him incapacitated, unfit for active service, they said. He never
ceased to amaze me though.'

'In what way?' asked Paddy.

'First and foremost, he never lost his sense of devilment or his
sense of humour. I could never understand how he managed to do
that, because medicine wasn't so advanced then as it is now, and he
was in constant pain. But mark my words, it didn't stop him getting around or doing the things that he wanted to do. He taught
himself how to play the fiddle, for example. He learned how to
read and write properly, which, he said himself, was a real miracle.
And to top it all, he got married to a nurse that was looking after
him in the army hospital in England.'

'So he got married before he came back home then?' Paddy said.

'No, no, not at all,' Dan laughed. 'For a number of years they
did their courting with love letters. Then out of the blue one day
Tommy told a neighbour that he had some unfinished business to
clear up in England. "Keep the bed aired for me", he said, "I'll be
back within the month".' Three weeks later, much to everyone's
surprise, he came back with a blushing bride on his arm.'

'Do you mean to tell us that no one knew that he was going
away to get married?' Paddy asked.

'Married? No one even knew that he was courting her by way
of the Royal Mail. But wait now till I tell you the best of it. They
weren't long hitched at the time when they came down to stay

with me for a few days, and when I got Tommy on his own for a while, I says to him, "Tommy, how did you go about persuading a grand girl like that to marry such a scallywag like you?" "Well, it's like this now, Dan", said he to me, "we were walking down along Brighton Pier holding hands, nattering about this and that. 'Helen', I says to her, 'does this mean that we're getting hitched and having a day?' 'I suppose it does, love', she said, 'aren't we going out steady for long enough?'"

'Well, that beats all, Dan.'

'It does, Paddy. Tommy Danagher died about five years ago and as far as I know she's in an old folks home somewhere in England.'

'What about that soldier there?' The Boy asked, pointing to the man with his tongue sticking out.

'Seamus Slattery. "Silence" we called him. Every time he told you something, no matter how trivial it was, he'd always put his finger to his lips and say, "don't tell anyone I told you that". He went over the top in the first wave at the battle of the Somme, and that was the last time we ever laid eyes on him. Missing in action, presumed dead. That was the phrase they had for lads who never came home. Missing in action. So there you are now, lad. At the end of the day there's only one survivor left from that tattered photograph there, and you're looking at him. Dan Franey, war veteran, bachelor, and lover of good dogs and fresh trout.'

'Ah God, Mr Franey, the trout! I nearly forgot the trout! Where's the scales?' Dan went into the scullery and they followed him in. The trout was put up on the brass scales and balanced and counter balanced with brass ingots until the correct weight was measured.

'What's in him, Dan?' Paddy asked.

'Let me see now.' Dan leaned down to view the pointer. 'Three quarters of a pound, to the exact ounce.'

'That scales must be banjaxed.' The Boy said earnestly. 'That trout is much heavier than that, so he is.'

'Look for yourself then,' Paddy said. The Boy bent down for a closer look at the scales, and was just in time to catch Dan take his forefinger away from the balance and see the needle spring up to register at two pounds fifteen ounces.

'Got you there!' said Dan.

The Boy looked from the trout to the scales. He grinned shyly and a little sheepishly and looked up at the two men.

'Got you there, my lad!' Dan said again, and all three of them filled the little kitchen with their laughter.

Chapter 16

Nodding and Lifting

The trout-angling season ended on the last day of September and fishing was out of bounds until the following March. It was a kind of waiting season but not an idle time. The long list of jobs posted on the Whelans' kitchen door was a breakfast-time reminder of all that needed to be done. Paddy and The Boy spent their time repairing fishing rods and landing-nets, and making up dozens of fishing flies for the next season. And fly-lines had to be attended to at the end of a busy fishing season. These were stripped from the reels and wound onto hard-wood spindles to dry, then treated with grease and put back on the reels.

But the lifting of the cot was the main task, a ritual that marked the high point of their quiet time. On the second Sunday of October, the cot would be solemnly lifted from the river and laid in dry dock for the winter months. Dry dock was nothing more than a ramshackle shed with three walls and a rusty galvanised roof, but it served them well for it had good space and ventilation, and the cot would dry out quickly there and be prepared for the coming season.

Lifting the cot was a grand affair and word-of-mouth elicited the goodwill and assistance of several key people. When things went according to plan there was a smooth transition from the water to the waiting lorry. The weather was crucial. If the river was in flood, it was extremely difficult to manoeuvre the cot into a convenient position in order to lift it. But if the river was low, the heavy cot had to be hauled up onto the high riverbank.

On Sunday morning the lifting crew began to sneak in through the back door of the Country Bar and Hotel. Prior arrangements were made with the landlady to facilitate their early arrival, but by eleven o'clock, the agreed quota of crew members had trebled in number.

'Secret my backside,' she said, referring to the clandestine nature of the agreement she'd made with Paddy. The bar-room was U-shaped. The counter-top was black and white flecked marble, with dark mahogany panels beneath. Over the years the owners had painted layer after layer of Van Dyke Brown stain onto the panels, and the entire surface area had ruptured into tiny cracks resembling the fine lines on a road map. The mixture of paint and grime reminded The Boy of a dresser he'd cleaned for the woman who lived just down the street from them. He talked himself into that job, stripped it down and painted it for her, and when it was finished it looked brand new. Maggie was pleased with the work, but said he'd have to wait for payment.

'Don't hold your breath,' Moll had said when he got home. 'You could smother and die twice over before you get that sixpence.'

He grinned ruefully at the memory. The counter looked very old and valuable and he thought about offering to strip it back. This time he'd settle for lots of crisps and red lemonade.

The world of the pub was new to The Boy and he was quite unprepared for the overpowering stench of stale porter and tobacco-smoke. The tall alcove window had clear glass at the top and translucent glass at the bottom. There were letters cut into the lower panes and he tried to read them backwards. The wooden seats along the walls and under the window sills looked the same as those in the local church except that they had cushions on them. Just as well, he thought, or they'd cut the arse off you.

Paddy sat up at the end of the counter and rested his back against the wall. Hill Sixteen, he called it, because he had a view over the entire bar and could see who was coming and going. One of the lifting crew came in and Paddy gave the landlady the nod. When he nodded she poured a drink and handed it over the counter to the client. The client nodded in return to acknowledge the drink. Then Paddy returned the nod, which in nodding language said that he was welcome to it. There was a lot of nodding that day.

Dykie Morrissey had been one of the first of the cot-lifters to arrive and he was standing at the far end of the counter, nursing the last quarter of a pint of stout and looking the worse for wear. The stout was like the blue-black elderberry ink in the Christian Brothers School, thin and diminished. Every time he sipped it, he shook himself and grimaced. The Boy looked from the stout to Dykie and felt a great surge of sympathy because the contents of the glass looked horrible and probably tasted even worse.

'Now there's a man that's suffering from high-stoolitis,' Paddy said, leaning down to hand his nephew a large bottle of red lemonade.

'What?'

'Never mind, Huck, never mind. Stick with the fizzy stuff and save your pennies to buy a chunk of the Mississippi for yourself,' Paddy said, and waved at Dykie to come and join him. The thin one picked up his glass and sauntered down the bar, then sat himself down on a stool at the outer limits of Hill Sixteen.

'How are you at all, my auld stock?' Paddy inquired, trying to hide a smile.

'Well, let me put it like this,' said Dykie. 'The young fella, Sean, came home from blighty early in the week, just a quick trip specially to see his mother, like. She was after having an operation on the auld water works because she was getting up four or five times during the night, every night like. Do you get my drift, Paddy?'

'Oh I do, Dykie, I certainly do.'

'Arra, she had no comfort at all, at all. It was that bad in the long run that when she coughed she wet her knickers. She ended up having to carry spares around in her handbag all the time, for emergencies like. Do you know what I mean, Paddy?'

Paddy almost gagged on his drink.

'Oh holy Mother of God, I do Dykie.'

'The head saw-doctor in the hospital told me himself that she was under the knife for two and half hours or more. "When you were poking around inside her", said I, "did you find a heart in there by any chance?" For some reason he didn't seem to catch the funny side of it. Anyway, he seemed to be a very dour, serious kind of quack altogether. I suppose you could get that way if you were rooting around in blood and guts every day of the week. It would be hard to see the funny side of things, know what I mean, like?'

'Will you stop it, Dykie, and have a pint, for God's sake,' Paddy laughed.

'I will Paddy, and thanks a lot. But as I was telling you, the young fella dagged home from London to see herself and he dragged me out last night for a few pints.'

'Well, well, well, isn't that a fright now,' said a voice behind him. 'I'm sure it was a major row to drag you out of the house and into a pub.'

Two more of the lifters made their way through the smokey dimness – The Whippet and The Battle.

'Hello men. How're things?' Paddy turned to greet them.

'God bless all within,' The Whippet said, and then looked directly into Dykie Morrissey's bloodshot eyes. 'Jasus Dykie, you're only a pale shadow of your former self. What in Christ's name happened to you? What did you do to yourself, my auld flower? You look shagging awful, so you do.'

'Well, for once you might be speaking the truth, Whippet, for I do feel a bit queasy – bloody awful in fact. But as I was explaining to Paddy before you so rudely interrupted, the son and myself went on a bit of a batter last night and to be perfectly honest, I'm as sick as a small hospital. Those last few half-ones did the damage, I think. Then, to add insult to injury, I've a pain in my fecking arm as well. I must've banged against a wall or something on the way home.'

The Whippet winked at the landlady.

'Give that poor man beside me there a large hair of the dog. I just couldn't bear to look at him in that state for the rest of the day. He reminds me of death warmed up, a terrible reminder of my own inevitable demise. It's a drop of Jamesons that he drinks. A great auld cure I'm told, better than any trip to Lourdes.'

'Thanks, I'll try it,' Dykie sighed. 'I'd try poison this very minute if I thought it would do any shagging good.'

'What's more,' the Whippet said, 'that pain in the arm you're moaning about, it's from lifting too many pint glasses.'

'Ah Jasus,' Dykie says lifting his eyes to the ceiling in prayer. 'I swear, I'm truly sorry for having offended thee and I promise never to offend thee again, but for fuck's sake, would you ever get that shagging Whippet off me back. He has the life pestered out of me. That fecking drink that he bought me won't be worth a curse until he fecking well shuts up. Amen.'

The lift was supposed to start at half-past eleven but the lorryman hadn't turned up and now the pub clock said half-past midday. The landlady came from inside the counter, squeezed her way past a group of men, and then opened the doors for official business.

'Come on now lads, drink up! Drink up now, it's opening time,' came the voice of a wag from the far corner. 'Don't you have no other pubs to go to?'

'The first one of you to put a foot outside that door before I say so will be barred instantly, for life,' Bridie said sternly.

'Well, feck it all, girlie' Jackie Kerrigan ran his fingers through his shock of grey hair. 'Most of the time you can't wait to see the back of us.'

'Now let me tell you, Mr Kerrigan, it's a long time since I was a little girl,' Bridie said, wagging a finger at him. 'I'll have you know that I'm an experienced, mature lady who wishes to be addressed in a manner suitable to her status.'

'There's no doubt about that, missus.' A man in a neat suit and well-pressed Dublin accent leaned against a pillar with a smirk on his face. 'Well rounded you surely are.'

'What do you mean by that, sir?' Bridie snapped.

'I mean that you're good at a lot of things, madam. But, personally speaking, at this moment in time, I can't comment on your upstairs performance unless you invite me up with you.'

'How dare you utter such smut! I have a good mind to ask you and your impertinence to leave. Who are you, my good man? I don't believe that I've seen you in my emporium before.'

The stranger scowled and his face turned a deep crimson.

'Never you mind who I am, missus marbles-in-the-mouth hoity-toity,' he snapped. 'I only slipped in here for a quick jar when I saw a few men going in the side door. But you're dead right, missus, you haven't seen me here before and you won't be seeing me here again.'

He planted his glass emphatically on the counter-top and made his way to the door.

'Emporium, my arse!' he said, by way of a parting-shot, and slammed the oak shut behind him.

The reverberations of the slammed door left an uneasy silence. All eyes tracked Bridie as she walked unhurriedly across the floor and in behind the counter. Three men, who were standing near the toilet entrance, sneaked inside. Hurricane Bridie was about to blow and they took shelter from the impending storm.

'Shagging cowards,' The Whippet muttered under his breath.

Everyone avoided Bridie's gaze and few dared to speak. She looked as if she was about to explode.

'I see,' she said, her gaze panning the entire clientele, and cowing them still further with a blast of withering sarcasm. 'Just look at you – all my knights in shining armour. Thank you, one and all, for standing up for me like gentlemen. After all that I've done for you over the years, not one of you had the gumption to tell that jumped-up Dublin jackeen where to get off!'

'I was going to give him a right good kick in the balls, Bridie, but I was too far away from him,' Jackie Kerrigan said. 'And anyway,' he added with biting sarcasm of his own, 'I didn't want to upset you or your, ah, emporium.'

'That's it, that's the last straw, Mr Kerrigan. Out. Get out now this very instant or I may have to come outside this counter and eject you myself." Bridie was fairly trembling with fury. 'It was you, Kerrigan, who started this whole sordid episode with your comments.'

Bridie scanned the faces up and down the bar for signs of support.

'Ah Bridie, Bridie, he didn't mean anything by it. You didn't, sure you didn't, Jackie? said a soothing voice from some dim-lit corner. A small ragged chorus of voices pleaded with the landlady.

'Ah go on, Bridie. Give him a chance'

'It was all that jackeen's fault, so it was.'

'He didn't mean it.'

Bridie hesitated, and Jackie took his cue.

'Indeed, I didn't mean to upset you, Bridie,' he said, cashing in on the moral support. 'I was only having a bit of a craic with you, winding you up, that's all. I'm sorry if I offended you.'

'Oh very well then, Mr Kerrigan,' Bridie relented. 'It goes against my better judgement, but I'll give you one last chance. But you'd better take care of your manners from here on in.' There was a general murmur of satisfaction and normal service was resumed.

The clock struck two and announced the end of Sunday morning opening hours. Bridie bolted the doors and nobody, including Kerrigan, had any intention of leaving. The holy hour came and went. Heads were nodded, elbows were exercised and everyone was happy except Paddy Whelan, who was growing more and more worried that the lorry-driver hadn't turned up despite several attempts to locate him.

'We'll give him till half-past three,' he said, reaching for the box of sandwiches that Moll had packed. He passed them round to the crew along with thick slices of fruit cake. They settled down to eat and drink, and time moved on.

'Will you give us a blast of a song, Dykie,' The Whippet said.

'Sure, I might as well.' Dykie readily agreed. 'It's too late to go home early, now.'

The Whippet winked across at Paddy. Obviously, the 'hair of the dog' had worked the oracle on Dykie.

'Give him your undivided attention, boys,' Bridie commanded, a little breathlessly. It was four o'clock. She had just reopened the door for official business, and bustled her way back inside the counter.

'She's right lads,' The Whippet said. 'Give him a chance now or he might take on his prima donna role and not oblige us at all.'

Thus encouraged, Dykie took a long swallow from the pint of stout, cleared his throat and began.

There was a wild colonial boy Jack Duggan was his name,
He was born and reared in Ireland in a place called Castlemaine,
He was his father's only son, his mother's pride and joy,
And dearly did his parents love the wild colonial boy.

Halfway through the song, two Guards came through the side door, elbowed their way into the corner at the far end of the bar, removed their caps, and settled at the counter for the long haul. More nodding was called for. Paddy gave Bridie the nod and she served them with two large bottles of stout. The sergeant lifted his glass and nodded to Paddy, who nodded back.

'Cushy won't be long training in the new recruit, Bridie,' Paddy said.

'You're right, Paddy.'

'While you're there, Bridie, hand me out that squeezebox. If you can't beat them, you might as well join them.' She reached under the counter and pulled out the accordion.

'Good on you, Paddy Whelan, you never let the side down yet,' said The Battle, nodding for another round. Dykie brought the 'Wild Colonial Boy' to a close and Paddy followed with 'The Isle of Inisfree.' The session was well under way now and still there was no sign of the lorry driver. The three-thirty deadline had long passed, and the mid-October light was fading fast outside.

'It's not like Seanie to let us down like this, Paddy,' Dykie said.

'No, it's not his style at all. He's usually bang on time when he has a job to do. Something must have happened. Anyway, it's gone too late to lift the cot now. The light will gone altogether in an hour or so.'

'We'll lift her next Sunday, so we will, Paddy, if I have to carry her up on my own back,' promised The Whippet.

'Jasus, drink is a mighty booster, or should I say boaster,' Dykie said. 'By the way, while you're in that form, give us the narration about the wreck.'

'If it's a wreck that you want, then look no further. Here's a man who's wrecked from a life of strife and hard labour slogging in ditches and drains. A man that's worked his arse off for the County Council for the last twenty years with little or no reward to show for it.'

'Do you know what, Whippet? My heart bleeds for you, so it does. Will you stop your auld whinging and get on with the recitation.'

'I'll give you "The Wreck of the *Gwendoline*",' Whippet said, 'and I'll ignore that snide remark from you, Morrissey. Please pass out the podium, Bridie.' Bridie picked up a red-painted butter box from inside the counter and handed it to The Whippet. He put it beside one of the pillars and then stood up on it where everyone could see him.

'The speaker has the floor,' shouted Bridie. The butter box was a gift from one of her customers who had spent some years living in London. He said that no less a personage than the Archbishop of Canterbury had used the box. As a boy, the Archbishop had had socialist tendencies, and he stood on the box to preach to the public at Speakers Corner in Hyde Park. Bridie half-believed the story but it didn't really matter whether it was true or not, because over the years the red box had acquired a status all of its own. It was clearly understood that whoever stood on it within the precincts of the bar commanded silence and attention. The Whippet stood on the box with an air of solemnity, and began.

'From the day I was nine, the wish was mine,
A sailor bold to be;
I began to pine for the stormy brine,
And a life on the deep blue sea,
And so one day on the old Bridge Quay,
I kissed my blue-eyed Nell
And I shipped with joy as a cabin boy
To a boatman of Clonmel.

'Tis a dreadful shock to leave Poulslough
When the heart is young and bright,
The street called Hawke, and Gravel Walk,
And Duckett Street by night.
My sweet abode on Kerry Road
Is shrined in memory's cell.

Ah, cruel fate! Goodbye, West Gate,
And Shambles Lane – farewell.'

The audience was enthralled with The Whippet's recitation, and his delivery. He gesticulated left, then right, then left again like a true thespian, and his voice had the timbre of drama. Halfway through the narrative, Jackie Kerrigan fell off his barstool. It happened in slow-motion, as though choreographed by something that seemed to say 'I know I'm going to fall off the stool, and I can't do a thing about, so, please God, let me do it gracefully without spilling any drink in the process'. Jackie's elbow skated along the counter immediately before he began a slow collapse towards the floor. Before he disappeared, one hand reached back for the counter top. The wrist slanted elegantly and positioned the pint on the counter without spilling one single drop of stout. The men who were standing beside Jackie caught him and then propped him against the bar again only seconds before Bridie turned around. Jackie looked the picture of sobriety with his elbow resting on the bar and his chin in the palm of his hand. He gave Bridie a big smile and then nodded.

'What a performance!' Dykie said to Paddy.

'What a performer!' Paddy replied.

'The morn was still near Hughes' mill
The Gwendoline *was moored*
We laid in grog, and a terrier dog,
And a cargo of oats – insured,
So we poled away at the break of day
And waved all friends adieu;
And a loud farewell rang the friary bell

As the brewery hove in view.'

The Whippet was building up to the finale. Then the door oppo-site Hill Sixteen opened and Seanie Sullivan, the elusive lorry dri-ver, walked in.

'Jasus lads, but ye have a mighty session going on here,' he said, rubbing his hands in delight. 'What's the occasion?'

'Quiet please, Mr Sullivan, The Whippet has the floor,' Bridie commanded.

The Whippet stopped his recitation in mid–flow.

'What did she say? Did she say Sullivan? Where is he? I'll give him the floor all right. He'll be stretched out on the floor if I can get my hands on him.' The Whippet forgot his party piece for the moment and rounded on the newcomer.

'What the hell do you mean by arriving at this shagging time of the day? It's half-past six in the evening! Just look at the fecking time on that clock.' Whippet said pointing animatedly at the clock behind the bar. The lorry-driver was taken aback by The Whippet's outburst.

'I know what time of the day it is, Mr Smartarse,' he said. 'What the hell are you so shagging fired up about? It's the same time at this time every Sunday and I come out every Sunday at this time. Is it because I missed the start of your gala performance that you're acting like a mad-hatter lunatic?'

'Well now, Mr Sullivan, what about your pledge to lift the cot?' The Whippet growled. 'What about the lorry you promised?'

'No problem auld stock, no problem at all,' Seanie Sullivan sniped back. 'That's all organised. I'll be here next Sunday at half-ten on the dot, as I promised.'

Any thespian worth his salt would have killed for the expression that passed across The Whippet's face as realisation dawned.

'Oh sweet divine Jasus,' he gasped. 'Give me patience. What kind of an eejit have we here at all? I'll go and finish my recitation.'

'He's right, Paddy. I'm an eejit,' the lorry-driver said. 'I thought it was next Sunday. I'm terrible sorry so I am, just look at all the trouble I've caused you.' He laid a hand on Paddy's shoulder.

'Trouble? What trouble, Seanie? Sure, we're having a great time here,' Paddy said. 'It was just a mix up, that's all. We'll see you next Sunday. You'll have a pint, Seanie?'

Bridie got the nod to pull the pint and The Whippet resumed his recitation.

'At the word "Avast" we manned each mast,
And we cheered for Murphy's stout,
As the cheer arose, we frightened the crows
On the starboard bow with the shout.'

'Huck, tell Moll when you get home that things didn't go to plan.' Paddy turned to The Boy. 'Tell her I'll be another while because we have a few more songs to murder.'

'Aw, can't I stay, Uncle Paddy?'

'No.' Paddy was emphatic. 'You have school in the morning, and anyway, if you drink any more lemonade, you'll burst.'

'But the day grew dark, and the bounding barque
Was struck by a sudden squall,
The Captain grew pale in the driving gale,
As we swept by the Gashouse Wall.'

'Oh, all right, so.' The Boy knew it was useless to argue with

Paddy when his mind was made up. 'Will I bring home the grappling hook and the food bag?'

'Just bring the bag, Huck.'

'Her timber creaks, and now she leaks;
With a shovel we try to bale,
But not even that, nor the captain's hat,
Nor an old top boot avail.
We neared the bank and threw a plank
To the Tipperary shore;
One whirl it gave, and then in the wave
It sank to rise no more.'

'Good luck, young fella.'

'See you next week, Mr Morrissey.' The Boy shouted above the din. 'We'll lift her then.'

'We will indeed, lad. We will indeed.'